Google JAX Cookbook

Perform machine learning and numerical computing with combined capabilities of TensorFlow and NumPy

Zephyr Quent

Published by: GitforGits

Publisher: Sonal Dhandre

www.gitforgits.com

support@gitforgits.com

Printed in India

First Printing: October 2024

ISBN: 978-81-979504-1-4

Cover Design by: Kitten Publishing

Prologue

As a machine learning engineer, I often found myself facing the limitations of NumPy. It was great for numerical computing, but when it came to scaling up models or training complex neural networks, it just couldn't keep up. The issue wasn't just about speed, though that was certainly a factor. I also had trouble with automatic differentiation and GPU acceleration, which made me look for alternatives that could handle the demands of modern machine learning workflows.

That's when I discovered Google JAX. JAX offered the potential for faster execution through just-in-time (JIT) compilation, and there were more benefits to come. It had built-in support for automatic differentiation and seamless integration with hardware acceleration, which made it an attractive option. As with any tool, there was a learning curve and a few hurdles to overcome. Moving from the familiar world of NumPy meant a change in mindset and code structure. A lot of people have trouble with this change, and I was no exception.

I was inspired to write the Google JAX Cookbook because I wanted to share practical solutions based on my own experiences with these challenges. I wanted to create something that was more than just a theoretical reference—I wanted to put together a hands-on, actionable book filled with practical recipes. Each recipe in this book tackles a specific issue, offers a clear solution, and provides enough context to make it useful without overwhelming you. I've put together the book in a way that takes you through different situations you might come across, from speeding up basic numerical operations to troubleshooting training issues.

In the book, I cover some of the challenges of profiling computation and memory, debugging runtime errors, and optimizing neural networks for different hardware setups. You'll also get tips on how to manage data structures with Pytrees, use JAX's Foreign Function Interface (FFI) to integrate external libraries, and even set up experiment tracking with Penzai to keep your projects organized. Each chapter builds on the last, gradually increasing in complexity while making sure you don't get lost along the way. I've kept a consistent focus on solving real-world problems because, at the end of the day, that's what matters.

One of the main things I focus on is showing you how to use JAX to your advantage. JAX's strength is its flexibility. Once you start to understand its nuances, you'll see it opens up a world of possibilities. You'll find tips on everything from switching from high-precision to mixed precision to speed up training to managing memory more effectively to prevent out-of-memory errors. All the techniques you need to get started right away.

I've written this book with data scientists, machine learning engineers, and AI practitioners in mind. If you're looking for ways to make your workflows faster, more efficient, and less prone to errors, this book is a great resource to have on hand. Together, we'll figure out how to use JAX, fix any problems that come up, and see what's possible with advanced machine learning.

Content

Preface

This is the practical, solution-oriented book data scientists, machine learning engineers, and AI engineers need to make the most of Google JAX for efficient and advanced machine learning. It covers essential tasks, troubleshooting scenarios, and optimization techniques to address common challenges encountered while working with JAX across machine learning and numerical computing projects.

The book starts with the move from NumPy to JAX. It introduces the best ways to speed up computations, handle data types, generate random numbers, and perform in-place operations. It then shows you how to use profiling techniques to monitor computation time and device memory, helping you to optimize training and performance. The debugging section provides clear and effective strategies for resolving common runtime issues, including shape mismatches, NaNs, and control flow errors.

The book goes on to show you how to master Pytrees for data manipulation, integrate external functions through the Foreign Function Interface (FFI), and utilize advanced serialization and type promotion techniques for stable computations. If you want to optimize training processes, this book has you covered. It includes recipes for efficient data loading, building custom neural networks, implementing mixed precision, and tracking experiments with Penzai. You'll learn how to visualize model performance and monitor metrics to assess training progress effectively. The recipes in this book tackle real-world scenarios and give users the power to fix issues and fine-tune models quickly.

In this book you will learn how to:

- Get your calculations done faster by moving from NumPy to JAX's optimized framework.
- Make your training pipelines more efficient by profiling how long things take and how much memory they use.
- Use debugging techniques to fix runtime issues like shape mismatches and numerical instability.
- Get to grips with Pytrees for managing complex, nested data structures across various machine learning tasks.
- Use JAX's Foreign Function Interface (FFI) to bring in external functions and give your computational capabilities a boost.
- Take advantage of mixed-precision training to speed up neural network computations without sacrificing model accuracy.
- Keep your experiments on track with Penzai. This lets you reproduce results and monitor key metrics.

- Use advanced visualization techniques, like confusion matrices and learning curves, to make model evaluation more effective.
- Create your own neural networks and optimizers directly in JAX so you have full control of the architecture.
- Use serialization techniques to save, load, and transfer models and training checkpoints efficiently.

GitforGits

Prerequisites

Every data scientist, machine learning engineer, AI practitioner, data engineers and statisticians must make use of Google JAX in their projects.

Codes Usage

Are you in need of some helpful code examples to assist you in your programming and documentation? Look no further! Our book offers a wealth of supplemental material, including code examples and exercises.

Not only is this book here to aid you in getting your job done, but you have our permission to use the example code in your programs and documentation. However, please note that if you are reproducing a significant portion of the code, we do require you to contact us for permission.

But don't worry, using several chunks of code from this book in your program or answering a question by citing our book and quoting example code does not require permission. But if you do choose to give credit, an attribution typically includes the title, author, publisher, and ISBN. For example, "Google JAX Cookbook by Zephyr Quent".

If you are unsure whether your intended use of the code examples falls under fair use or the permissions outlined above, please do not hesitate to reach out to us at support@gitforgits.com.

We are happy to assist and clarify any concerns.

Acknowledgement

I owe a tremendous debt of gratitude to GitforGits, for their unflagging enthusiasm and wise counsel throughout the entire process of writing this book. Their knowledge and careful editing helped make sure the piece was useful for people of all reading levels and comprehension skills. In addition, I'd like to thank everyone involved in the publishing process for their efforts in making this book a reality. Their efforts, from copyediting to advertising, made the project what it is today.

Finally, I'd like to express my gratitude to everyone who has shown me unconditional love and encouragement throughout my life. Their support was crucial to the completion of this book. I appreciate your help with this endeavour and your continued interest in my career.

CHAPTER 1: TRANSITION NUMPY TO JAX

Overview

Moving from NumPy to JAX opens up new possibilities for machine learning engineers and data scientists, offering significant improvements in computational speed and efficiency. This chapter aims to ease this transition by addressing common challenges and introducing key concepts in JAX. The focus is on leveraging the advanced features of JAX while maintaining the familiarity of NumPy's syntax and operations, allowing you to improve performance without a steep learning curve.

In this chapter, we will explore five key topics. First, we examine how to speed up existing NumPy code using JAX's just-in-time compilation and automatic differentiation. Next, we address the issue of unsupported NumPy functions in JAX and discover suitable alternatives for preserving functionality. We discuss effective management strategies for random number generation, as it differs in JAX compared to NumPy, to ensure reproducibility and reliability. The challenges posed by in-place operations require a different approach in JAX, which we will address to help you adapt your coding practices. Finally, we will explore JAX's type promotion semantics and precision handling to maintain numerical stability during the transition.

To provide a practical context, we will introduce the Fashion-MNIST dataset. This is a collection of grayscale images representing various clothing items. This dataset serves as an excellent testbed for building and optimizing machine learning models. Throughout the book, we use it to implement examples and exercises that allow you to apply the concepts you learn in real-world scenarios. Our hope is that your work with Fashion-MNIST will deepen your understanding of JAX while developing skills that are directly applicable to your own projects.

Accelerating NumPy Code with JAX

The Fashion-MNIST dataset consists of 70,000 grayscale images of various fashion items such as T-shirts, trousers, and shoes. Each image is 28x28 pixels and belongs to one of ten classes. The dataset is available to download at https://github.com/zalandoresearch/fashion-mnist. While NumPy is a powerful library for numerical computations, using it to train machine learning models on large datasets like Fashion-MNIST can be inefficient and slow. The lack of just-in-time (JIT) compilation and automatic differentiation means computations are interpreted at runtime, and gradients must be calculated manually. The challenge is to accelerate existing NumPy code to efficiently handle large-scale computations involved in training neural networks on the Fashion-MNIST dataset.

To overcome the performance limitations of NumPy, we can leverage Google JAX. By converting existing NumPy code to JAX, significant speedups in computation can be achieved, and gradient calculations can be simplified. This involves replacing NumPy imports with JAX's NumPy and applying JIT compilation and automatic differentiation to the code.

Setting up Environment

First, ensure that JAX is installed in your Python environment:

```
pip install --upgrade "jax[cpu]"
```

Loading Fashion-MNIST Dataset

The TensorFlow Datasets library provides an easy interface to access standard datasets like Fashion-MNIST. Follow the below steps:

```
import tensorflow_datasets as tfds

# Load the dataset

data = tfds.load('fashion_mnist', split=['train',
'test'], as_supervised=True)

train_data, test_data = data
```

Preprocessing Data

Next, you preprocess the images and labels to prepare them for training. To do this, normalize the images and convert them to NumPy arrays.

```
import numpy as np

def preprocess(image, label):

    image = np.array(image) / 255.0  # Normalize pixel
values

    image = image.reshape(-1)         # Flatten the image

    label = np.array(label)

    return image, label

# Convert the dataset to NumPy arrays
```

```
train_images = []
train_labels = []
for image, label in tfds.as_numpy(train_data):
    img, lbl = preprocess(image, label)
    train_images.append(img)
    train_labels.append(lbl)
train_images = np.array(train_images)
train_labels = np.array(train_labels)
```

Building a Simple Neural Network with NumPy

Now, create a simple neural network with one hidden layer using NumPy.

```
# Initialize parameters
input_size = 784  # 28x28 pixels flattened
hidden_size = 128
output_size = 10   # 10 classes
np.random.seed(0)
W1 = np.random.randn(input_size, hidden_size) * 0.01
b1 = np.zeros((1, hidden_size))
W2 = np.random.randn(hidden_size, output_size) * 0.01
b2 = np.zeros((1, output_size))
# Activation functions
def relu(x):
```

```
    return np.maximum(0, x)

def softmax(x):

    exp_x = np.exp(x - np.max(x, axis=1, keepdims=True))
# Stability improvement

    return exp_x / np.sum(exp_x, axis=1, keepdims=True)
```

Defining Forward and Backward Passes

Once created, implement the forward pass and compute the loss.

```
def forward_pass(x):

    z1 = np.dot(x, W1) + b1

    a1 = relu(z1)

    z2 = np.dot(a1, W2) + b2

    y_pred = softmax(z2)

    return y_pred, a1

def compute_loss(y_pred, y_true):

    m = y_true.shape[0]

    log_likelihood = -np.log(y_pred[range(m), y_true])

    loss = np.sum(log_likelihood) / m

    return loss
```

Implement the backward pass to compute gradients manually.

```
def backward_pass(x, a1, y_pred, y_true):

    global W1, b1, W2, b2
```

```
    m = y_true.shape[0]

    y_true_one_hot = np.zeros_like(y_pred)
    y_true_one_hot[np.arange(m), y_true] = 1
    dz2 = y_pred - y_true_one_hot
    dW2 = np.dot(a1.T, dz2) / m
    db2 = np.sum(dz2, axis=0, keepdims=True) / m
    da1 = np.dot(dz2, W2.T)
    dz1 = da1 * (a1 > 0)
    dW1 = np.dot(x.T, dz1) / m
    db1 = np.sum(dz1, axis=0, keepdims=True) / m
    # Update parameters
    learning_rate = 0.01
    W1 -= learning_rate * dW1
    b1 -= learning_rate * db1
    W2 -= learning_rate * dW2
    b2 -= learning_rate * db2
```

Training Model

Now, its time to train the model using the manual forward and backward passes.

```
num_epochs = 5
batch_size = 64
```

```
for epoch in range(num_epochs):
    permutation =
np.random.permutation(train_images.shape[0])
    train_images_shuffled = train_images[permutation]
    train_labels_shuffled = train_labels[permutation]

    for i in range(0, train_images.shape[0], batch_size):
        x_batch = train_images_shuffled[i:i+batch_size]
        y_batch = train_labels_shuffled[i:i+batch_size]

        y_pred, a1 = forward_pass(x_batch)
        loss = compute_loss(y_pred, y_batch)
        backward_pass(x_batch, a1, y_pred, y_batch)

    print(f"Epoch {epoch+1}, Loss: {loss}")
```

It is also observed that training the model using NumPy can be slow due to the manual computation of gradients and the absence of JIT compilation. The execution time increases significantly with larger datasets and more complex models, making it impractical for large-scale machine learning tasks.

Converting NumPy Code to JAX

To accelerate the code, convert it to use JAX. This involves importing JAX's NumPy and utilizing its JIT compilation and automatic differentiation features. To do this, replace NumPy imports with JAX's NumPy and import necessary JAX functions.

```
import jax.numpy as jnp
```

```
from jax import grad, jit, random
from functools import partial
```

After this, update the activation functions and model functions to use JAX's NumPy.

```
# Initialize parameters with JAX
key = random.PRNGKey(0)
W1 = random.normal(key, (input_size, hidden_size)) * 0.01
b1 = jnp.zeros((1, hidden_size))
W2 = random.normal(key, (hidden_size, output_size)) *
0.01
b2 = jnp.zeros((1, output_size))
def relu(x):
    return jnp.maximum(0, x)
def softmax(x):
    exp_x = jnp.exp(x - jnp.max(x, axis=1,
keepdims=True))
    return exp_x / jnp.sum(exp_x, axis=1, keepdims=True)
```

Then, define the loss function using JAX.

```
def compute_loss(params, x, y):
    W1, b1, W2, b2 = params
    z1 = jnp.dot(x, W1) + b1
    a1 = relu(z1)
```

```
    z2 = jnp.dot(a1, W2) + b2
    y_pred = softmax(z2)
    m = y.shape[0]
    log_likelihood = -jnp.log(y_pred[jnp.arange(m), y])
    loss = jnp.sum(log_likelihood) / m
    return loss
```

Next, use JAX's **grad** function to compute gradients automatically.

```
grad_loss = grad(compute_loss)
```

After that, apply JIT compilation to the training step function.

```
@jit
def update(params, x, y, learning_rate=0.01):
    grads = grad_loss(params, x, y)
    params = [param - learning_rate * grad for param,
grad in zip(params, grads)]
    return params
```

And finally, train the model using the optimized JAX functions.

```
params = [W1, b1, W2, b2]
num_epochs = 5
batch_size = 64
for epoch in range(num_epochs):
```

```
    permutation =
np.random.permutation(train_images.shape[0])
    train_images_shuffled = train_images[permutation]
    train_labels_shuffled = train_labels[permutation]

    for i in range(0, train_images.shape[0], batch_size):
        x_batch = train_images_shuffled[i:i+batch_size]
        y_batch = train_labels_shuffled[i:i+batch_size]
        params = update(params, x_batch, y_batch)

    current_loss = compute_loss(params, x_batch, y_batch)
    print(f"Epoch {epoch+1}, Loss: {current_loss}")
```

By converting the code to JAX and utilizing automatic differentiation and JIT compilation, significant speedups in training time are achieved. The use of **`grad`** simplifies gradient computations, and the **`@jit`** decorator accelerates the execution of the training loop. Additionally, JAX operations are designed to run efficiently on CPUs, GPUs, and TPUs. This makes it feasible to experiment with more complex models or larger datasets.

By following this approach, existing NumPy code can be effectively accelerated using Google JAX, enabling efficient handling of large-scale computations and complex machine learning models on datasets like Fashion-MNIST.

Handling Unsupported NumPy Functions in JAX

When transitioning from NumPy to Google JAX, certain NumPy functions may not be available in JAX's NumPy API (**`jax.numpy`**), leading to compatibility issues. Functions like **`np.random.shuffle`**, **`np.linalg.eig`**, and some in-place operations are not directly supported in JAX due to its emphasis on functional programming and immutability. The goal is to find alternative methods or workarounds to replace unsupported NumPy functions in JAX while maintaining the original functionality of the code.

Suppose we have a NumPy-based implementation of a neural network that uses **np.random.shuffle** to shuffle the training data before each epoch. In JAX, **jax.random** does not have a direct equivalent of **np.random.shuffle** due to its functional programming design. We need to find an alternative way to shuffle the data in JAX.

Identifying Unsupported Functions

First, identify the functions in the NumPy code that are not supported in JAX. Following are the common unsupported functions:

- In-place operations (e.g., **np.random.shuffle**)
- Certain linear algebra functions (e.g., **np.linalg.eig**)
- Functions that rely on mutation or side effects

Replacing 'np.random.shuffle'

In the original NumPy code, data shuffling might be performed as:

```
np.random.shuffle(train_images)

np.random.shuffle(train_labels)
```

This in-place shuffling is not compatible with JAX's functional approach. Instead, we can use JAX's **random.permutation** function to achieve the same effect without in-place mutation.

Using JAX's 'random.permutation'

```
from jax import random

# Assume 'key' is a PRNGKey initialized earlier

key, subkey = random.split(key)

permutation = random.permutation(subkey,
train_images.shape[0])

train_images_shuffled = train_images[permutation]
```

```
train_labels_shuffled = train_labels[permutation]
```

Here, **random.permutation** generates a permutation of indices, which we use to index into the training data arrays, effectively shuffling them. This method avoids in-place operations and adheres to JAX's functional programming style.

Replacing unsupported Linear Algebra Functions

Suppose the code relies on **np.linalg.eig** to compute eigenvalues and eigenvectors, which is not available in **jax.numpy.linalg**. Then, we need an alternative approach such as:

- For symmetric or Hermitian matrices, **eigh** can be used instead of **eig**.
- Create custom functions to approximate eigenvalues and eigenvectors.
- Use singular value decomposition (**svd**), which is supported in JAX.

Following is a quick example of replacement using SVD:

```
# Original NumPy code

eigenvalues, eigenvectors = np.linalg.eig(matrix)

# JAX replacement

u, s, vh = jnp.linalg.svd(matrix)
```

The use of singular value decomposition allows for the acquisition of analogous insights into the characteristics of the matrix, without recourse to the unsupported eig function.

Handling In-Place Operations

The in-place operations are common in NumPy but are incompatible with JAX. For example:

```
# NumPy in-place operation

array *= scale_factor
```

Here, we need to avoid modifying arrays in place. Instead, we can perform the operation and assign the result to a new variable.

```
array = array * scale_factor
```

By reassigning the result to **array**, we maintain the functional programming paradigm of JAX.

Dealing with Advanced Indexing and Assignment

Suppose the code uses advanced indexing to modify array elements based on a condition:

```
# NumPy code

array[array > threshold] = new_value
```

We can use the **jax.numpy.where** function to achieve the same result without in-place modification.

```
array = jnp.where(array > threshold, new_value, array)
```

This creates a new array where elements satisfying the condition are replaced with **new_value**, while others remain unchanged.

Handling Random Number Generation Functions

Certain random number generation functions in NumPy do not have direct equivalents in JAX. For example, **np.random.choice** is used to select random samples from an array. In JAX, we can achieve similar functionality using available random functions.

Following is a quick example:

```
# NumPy code

samples = np.random.choice(array, size=sample_size,
replace=False)

# JAX replacement

key, subkey = random.split(key)

indices = random.choice(subkey, array.shape[0],
shape=(sample_size,), replace=False)

samples = array[indices]
```

By generating random indices using **random.choice**, we can select random samples from the array without directly using **np.random.choice**.

Implementing Custom Functions

If no direct replacement exists, we may need to implement custom functions compatible with JAX. For example, if we need a function to compute the matrix exponential, which is not available in JAX, we can create a custom implementation as below:

```
def matrix_exponential(a):

    # Simple implementation using the Padé approximant

    identity = jnp.eye(a.shape[0])

    a2 = jnp.dot(a, a)

    a4 = jnp.dot(a2, a2)

    numerator = identity + a + (1/2)*a2 +
(1/6)*jnp.dot(a2, a)

    denominator = identity - a + (1/2)*a2 -
(1/6)*jnp.dot(a2, a)

    exp_a = jnp.dot(jnp.linalg.inv(denominator),
numerator)

    return exp_a
```

The above one is a simplified example. For production code, I suggest to consider more robust implementations or libraries.

Using Third-Party Libraries Compatible with JAX

There are some libraries that extend JAX's functionality and provide additional features such as **jax.scipy** that offers scientific computing functions which are not available in **jax.numpy**.

Following is a quick example using jax.scipy:

```
from jax.scipy.linalg import expm

# Compute the matrix exponential
```

```
exp_a = expm(matrix)
```

With the above, we can access functions like **`expm`** for computing matrix exponentials.

Refactoring Code to Align with JAX's Paradigm

There are functions that rely on side effects or global state need to be refactored. For example, consider a function that updates a global counter:

```
counter = 0

def increment_counter(x):

    global counter

    counter += 1

    return x + counter
```

This above function is incompatible with JAX's transformations. Instead, we can pass the counter as an argument and return the updated value as demonstrated below.

```
def increment_counter(x, counter):

    counter += 1

    return x + counter, counter
```

By avoiding global state and side effects, the function becomes compatible with JAX's JIT compilation and automatic differentiation.

The deployment of these strategies enables the effective management of unsupported NumPy functions in JAX, ensuring the preservation of the original code's functionality while capitalizing on JAX's performance enhancements.

Managing Random Number Generation

In NumPy, randomness is managed through a global random state, which can lead to non-deterministic behavior if not handled carefully. Google JAX, however, adopts a different approach to random number generation, emphasizing functional purity and explicit state management. This difference can create uncertainty for those transitioning from NumPy, making it challenging to generate reproducible results. The task is to understand JAX's method of handling randomness using PRNG (Pseudo-Random Number Generator) keys and to learn how to use these keys effectively to ensure consistent and reproducible outcomes in experiments involving the Fashion-MNIST dataset.

Understanding JAX's PRNG Keys

In JAX, randomness is handled through the **`jax.random`** module, which provides functions for generating random numbers. These functions require a PRNG key as an input, and they return both the random numbers and new PRNG keys for subsequent use. The PRNG key is a **`jax.random.PRNGKey`** object that encapsulates the random state. By explicitly managing these keys, we are able to maintain control over the randomness inherent to our computations.

Initializing PRNG Key

The initial step is to import JAX's random module and initialize a PRNG key using a seed value. The seed value guarantees the generation of the identical sequence of random numbers across multiple runs.

```
import jax

from jax import random

# Initialize a PRNG key with a seed

seed = 42

key = random.PRNGKey(seed)
```

This key will be used to generate random numbers throughout the program. The seed value can be any integer and serves as the starting point for the random number generator.

Generating Random Numbers

The PRNG key should be employed for the generation of random numbers. For example, this may be employed to initialize model parameters or to create random permutations of data.

```
# Generating random weights for model initialization

key, subkey = random.split(key)
```

```
W = random.normal(subkey, shape=(input_size,
hidden_size)) * 0.01

# Generating random biases

key, subkey = random.split(key)

b = random.normal(subkey, shape=(hidden_size,)) * 0.01
```

In this code, **random.split** is used to split the key into two new keys: one for generating random numbers and one to be used for future operations.

Shuffling Data without In-Place Operations

Now when shuffling data, it's important to avoid in-place operations. So here, use JAX's **random.permutation** function with the PRNG key.

```
# Shuffling training data

key, subkey = random.split(key)

perm = random.permutation(subkey, train_images.shape[0])

train_images_shuffled = train_images[perm]

train_labels_shuffled = train_labels[perm]
```

The generation of a random permutation of indices enables the rearrangement of data arrays without modifying them in place. This approach aligns with JAX's functional programming methodology and ensures the reproducibility of results.

Ensuring Reproducibility in Model Training

It is recommended that the PRNG key be incorporated into functions that involve randomness in order to ensure reproducibility. So to illustrate, when defining the training step function, the key should be passed as an argument as shown below:

```
@jit

def train_step(params, x, y, key, learning_rate=0.01):
```

```
    key, subkey = random.split(key)

    # Use subkey for any randomness within the function

    loss, grads = compute_loss_and_grads(params, x, y,
subkey)

    params = [param - learning_rate * grad for param,
grad in zip(params, grads)]

    return params, key
```

The key is passed into the function and the updated key is returned, thereby maintaining control of the random state. This methodology guarantees that each training phase is deterministic when the same inputs are employed.

Using PRNG Keys in Data Augmentation

The process of data augmentation frequently entails the implementation of random transformations. The PRNG key should be employed in order to ensure the consistent application of these transformations.

```
def augment_data(x, key):

    key, subkey = random.split(key)

    # Apply random rotation

    angle = random.uniform(subkey, minval=-0.1,
maxval=0.1)

    x_rotated = rotate_image(x, angle)

    return x_rotated, key
```

Here, **rotate_image** is a hypothetical function that rotates the image by a given angle. By passing the key and updating it, we ensure that the randomness is controlled and reproducible.

Managing PRNG Keys in Loops

When using loops, update the PRNG key at each iteration to prevent reuse and maintain randomness.

```
key = random.PRNGKey(seed)

params = initialize_params(key)

for epoch in range(num_epochs):

    key, subkey = random.split(key)

    train_images_shuffled, train_labels_shuffled =
shuffle_data(train_images, train_labels, subkey)


    for batch in get_batches(train_images_shuffled,
train_labels_shuffled, batch_size):

        x_batch, y_batch = batch

        key, subkey = random.split(key)

        params, key = train_step(params, x_batch,
y_batch, subkey)
```

By consistently updating the key, we prevent accidental reuse, which could compromise the randomness and reproducibility of the results.

Incorporating PRNG Keys with JIT Compilation

Now when functions are compiled with **`@jit`**, special care must be taken with PRNG keys because JIT-compiled functions cache their results based on input shapes and types.

```
@jit

def compute_loss_and_grads(params, x, y, key):

    y_pred = model_forward(params, x)

    loss = cross_entropy_loss(y_pred, y)
```

```
    grads = grad(loss_fn)(params, x, y)
    return loss, grads
```

Since **key** is an input, the function will recompile if the key's value changes. To avoid excessive recompilation, structure your code to minimize changes in the key's shape and type.

Storing and Restoring PRNG Keys

If you need to pause and resume experiments, store the PRNG key along with model parameters to maintain reproducibility.

```
# Saving the state
state = {'params': params, 'key': key}
save_checkpoint(state, filename)
# Restoring the state
state = load_checkpoint(filename)
params = state['params']
key = state['key']
```

By saving the key, you ensure that the random state is preserved across sessions.

Using 'jax.random.fold_in' for Multi-Process Environments

In distributed or multi-process settings, use **jax.random.fold_in** to create unique keys for each process.

```
process_id = get_process_id()
key = random.PRNGKey(seed)
key = random.fold_in(key, process_id)
```

This method incorporates the process ID into the key, generating distinct random number sequences for each process while maintaining reproducibility.

By developing an understanding of and implementing effective management strategies for PRNG keys in JAX, it is possible to guarantee the reproducibility and consistency of machine learning experiments. This tactic serves to enhance the reliability of the results obtained, while simultaneously facilitating the debugging and verification processes inherent to projects involving the Fashion-MNIST dataset.

Dealing with In-Place Operations

In the process of migrating code from NumPy to Google JAX for the purpose of processing the dataset, one may potentially encounter challenges related to in-place operations. The original NumPy code may have been designed with a focus on direct array modification for efficiency, such as updating weights or applying transformations in place. However, this is due to the fact that JAX does not support in-place operations, which is a result of its functional programming paradigm that emphasises immutability and pure functions. This means operations like **`array *= scalar`** or **`array[index] = value`** are incompatible with JAX's just-in-time compilation and automatic differentiation. The challenge lies in refactoring the existing code to eliminate in-place operations while maintaining functionality and performance.

To resolve this issue, the code must be refactored in order to eliminate in-place operations. This can be achieved by adopting functional programming techniques. This requires that functions be rewritten in a manner that circumvents side effects and returns new arrays in lieu of modifying existing ones. As a result, the code becomes compatible with JAX's requirements, thereby enabling the use of JIT compilation and automatic differentiation. It is essential to exercise meticulous attention to the manner in which data is conveyed and modified, with the objective of maintaining the integrity of each function as a pure and stateless entity.

Understanding In-Place Operations and JAX's Paradigm

In-place operations modify the data directly, changing the state of variables or arrays. Examples include assignments like **`array += value`** or element-wise updates such as **`array[i] = new_value`**. In contrast, functional programming promotes immutability, where data is not altered after it's created. Functions return new data structures based on the input, without side effects. JAX adheres to this paradigm to facilitate powerful transformations and optimizations.

Consider a neural network training loop, where parameter updates are performed in place:

```
# Original NumPy code with in-place updates

for param, grad in zip(params, grads):

    param -= learning_rate * grad
```

This code modifies **param** directly, which is not allowed in JAX. Attempting to use this in-place operation will result in an error.

Refactored Code using Functional Updates

To refactor the code, we create a function that computes the updated parameters without modifying the originals:

```
# JAX-compatible code without in-place updates

def update_params(params, grads, learning_rate):

    return [param - learning_rate * grad for param, grad
in zip(params, grads)]
```

In the training loop, we reassign the parameters using the returned list:

```
# Training loop with functional updates

params = initialize_params()

for epoch in range(num_epochs):

    for x_batch, y_batch in data_loader:

        grads = compute_gradients(params, x_batch,
y_batch)

        params = update_params(params, grads,
learning_rate)
```

By avoiding in-place modifications, the code complies with JAX's functional approach.

Handling In-Place Array Modifications

Suppose we need to normalize data by subtracting the mean and dividing by the standard deviation, modifying the array in place:

```
# In-place normalization (NumPy code)

data -= data.mean(axis=0)
```

```
data /= data.std(axis=0)
```

Then, refactor this code to avoid in-place operations:

```
# JAX-compatible normalization
def normalize(data):
    mean = data.mean(axis=0)
    std = data.std(axis=0)
    return (data - mean) / std
normalized_data = normalize(data)
```

After that, by returning a new array, we maintain immutability.

Refactoring Conditional In-Place Updates

In cases where elements are conditionally updated, such as clipping values:

```
# In-place clipping (NumPy code)
weights[weights > max_value] = max_value
```

Use JAX's functional operations:

```
# JAX-compatible clipping
weights = jnp.minimum(weights, max_value)
```

Or, using **`jax.numpy.where`**:

```
weights = jnp.where(weights > max_value, max_value,
weights)
```

These methods create a new array without modifying the original.

Avoiding In-Place Accumulations

In algorithms involving accumulations, such as summing gradients:

```
# In-place accumulation (NumPy code)

total_grad += batch_grad
```

We refactor the above to:

```
# Functional accumulation

total_grad = total_grad + batch_grad
```

Alternatively, use reduction functions:

```
# Summing over a list of gradients

total_grad = jnp.sum(grads_list, axis=0)
```

Using 'jax.ops.index_update' for Indexing Updates

For updating specific indices, the deprecated **jax.ops.index_update** has been replaced with the **at** method:

```
# Original in-place indexing update (NumPy code)

array[index] = value

# JAX-compatible update

array = array.at[index].set(value)
```

This returns a new array with the specified update.

Refactoring Loops with In-Place Modifications

Consider a loop that modifies an array in place:

```
# In-place modification in loop (NumPy code)
```

```
for i in range(len(array)):
    array[i] *= scale_factors[i]
```

Now refactor it using functional programming:

```
# JAX-compatible code
scaled_array = array * scale_factors
```

By utilizing vectorized operations, we eliminate the need for explicit loops and in-place modifications.

By systematically refactoring the code in question, the in situ operations may be eliminated, thereby allowing for the full utilisation of Google JAX's features for machine learning projects. This approach guarantees that the resulting code is both efficient and scalable, and it aligns with modern practices in functional programming.

Ensuring Numerical Stability During Transition

After migrating a machine learning model from NumPy to Google JAX for the Fashion-MNIST dataset, numerical instability issues have been observed. These issues manifest as unexpected **`NaN`** (Not a Number) or infinite values during computations, which can halt training or produce incorrect results. Such instability may arise due to differences in how JAX handles data types and arithmetic operations compared to NumPy. Specifically, JAX's type promotion semantics can lead to unintended data type conversions, affecting the precision and stability of calculations. The challenge is to understand these differences and manage data types effectively to ensure stable and reliable computations in JAX.

In order to address the issue of numerical instability that has been observed subsequent to the transition to JAX, it is essential to have a clear understanding of the type promotion semantics employed by JAX and how these differ from the behaviour exhibited by NumPy. The numerical stability of computations may be achieved by the management of data types in an explicit manner, with the guarantee of consistent precision. This procedure entails an examination of the data types associated with arrays and variables, the designation of appropriate data types when required, and a cautious approach to operations that may result in unintended type promotions.

Understanding JAX's Type Promotion Semantics

JAX follows specific rules for type promotion during arithmetic operations, which can differ from NumPy's rules. In JAX, operations involving mixed precision can result in upcasting to higher precision types, potentially leading to increased memory usage and precision issues. For example, combining a **float32** array with a **float64** scalar may promote the result to **float64**, affecting computational efficiency and stability.

Inspecting Data Types

The initial step is to ascertain the data types of all input arrays and variables that are involved in computations. It is essential to guarantee that these values are of the desired precision, which is typically float32 for neural networks.

```
import jax.numpy as jnp

# Inspect data types

print(f"Data type of training images:
{train_images.dtype}")

print(f"Data type of training labels:
{train_labels.dtype}")
```

If the data types are not as expected, convert them explicitly.

Converting Data Types Explicitly

Next, convert arrays to the desired data type using **astype**.

```
# Convert data types to float32

train_images = train_images.astype(jnp.float32)

test_images = test_images.astype(jnp.float32)

# Convert labels to int32 if necessary

train_labels = train_labels.astype(jnp.int32)

test_labels = test_labels.astype(jnp.int32)
```

Initializing Model Parameters with Consistent Types

Now, when initializing model parameters such as weights and biases, you need to specify the data type to ensure consistency.

```
from jax import random

key = random.PRNGKey(seed)

# Initialize weights and biases with float32 data type

W1 = random.normal(key, (input_size, hidden_size),
dtype=jnp.float32) * 0.01

b1 = jnp.zeros((hidden_size,), dtype=jnp.float32)

W2 = random.normal(key, (hidden_size, output_size),
dtype=jnp.float32) * 0.01

b2 = jnp.zeros((output_size,), dtype=jnp.float32)
```

Ensuring Consistent Data Types in Computations

Here, in the model's forward pass and loss computations, ensure that operations are performed with consistent data types.

```
def forward_pass(params, x):

    W1, b1, W2, b2 = params

    x = x.astype(jnp.float32)

    z1 = jnp.dot(x, W1) + b1

    a1 = relu(z1)

    z2 = jnp.dot(a1, W2) + b2

    y_pred = softmax(z2)

    return y_pred
```

Handling Division and Logarithmic Operations

It is important to exercise caution when performing operations such as division and logarithms, as they can potentially introduce numerical instability if not handled correctly. It is advisable to add minor constants (ε) to the denominators or arguments of logarithms in order to preclude division by zero or the calculation of the logarithm of zero.

```
epsilon = 1e-7

def compute_loss(params, x, y):

    y_pred = forward_pass(params, x)

    m = y.shape[0]

    y_pred = jnp.clip(y_pred, epsilon, 1.0 - epsilon)

    log_likelihood = -jnp.log(y_pred[jnp.arange(m), y])

    loss = jnp.mean(log_likelihood)

    return loss
```

Now here, be cautious with operations that involve literals or constants. For example, dividing by an integer literal can cause unintended type promotion.

```
# Potential unintended promotion to float64

result = array / 255

# Corrected to maintain float32

result = array / 255.0
```

Ensure that constants are specified as floats when necessary.

Using JAX's Type Promotion Rules and Monitoring NaNs

Understand that JAX promotes types based on certain rules. For instance, operations between **`float16`** and **`float32`** promote to **`float32`**. Use this knowledge to control the precision of computations.

```
# Ensuring operations stay in float32

array1 = array1.astype(jnp.float32)

array2 = array2.astype(jnp.float32)

result = array1 + array2
```

After computations, check for the presence of **NaN** or infinite values, which indicate numerical instability.

```
# Checking for NaNs and infinities

if jnp.isnan(loss) or jnp.isinf(loss):

    print("Numerical instability detected in loss computation.")
```

If detected, investigate the preceding computations to identify the source.

Implementing Gradient Clipping

During training, large gradients can cause updates that lead to numerical instability. Apply gradient clipping to limit the magnitude of gradients.

```
from jax import tree_util

def clip_grads(grads, max_norm):

    total_norm = jnp.sqrt(sum([jnp.sum(jnp.square(g)) for g in tree_util.tree_leaves(grads)]))

    clip_coef = jnp.minimum(1.0, max_norm / (total_norm + 1e-6))

    grads = tree_util.tree_map(lambda g: g * clip_coef, grads)

    return grads
```

```
# Applying gradient clipping during the update
grads = grad_loss(params, x_batch, y_batch)
grads = clip_grads(grads, max_norm=1.0)
```

If numerical instability persists, consider using higher precision data types like **float64** for critical computations. However, be aware that this increases memory usage and computation time.

```
# Using float64 for critical computations
x = x.astype(jnp.float64)
```

To ensure consistency, it is imperative that all related variables be converted to float64.

Summary

In summary, this chapter focused on the transition from NumPy to Google JAX for machine learning tasks. It began by demonstrating how to accelerate existing NumPy code by converting to JAX using just-in-time compilation and automatic differentiation. This resulted in significant performance gains, allowing faster neural network training without having to re-write the code. Next, the challenges posed by unsupported NumPy functions in JAX were addressed. We also looked at old-fashioned ways of replacing these functions while still preserving the original functionality of the code. This way, compatibility was ensured and a seamless integration of JAX into existing workflows was possible.

An important topic was JAX's random generation, which differs from NumPy. Here we were able to learn about the effective use of PRNG keys and the reproducibility of results. We also tackled the problem of in-place operations. These are not supported in JAX due to its functional programming paradigm. The code was refactored to eliminate these operations, adopting a style that avoids side effects and emphasizes immutability. This refactoring not only made the code compatible with JAX, but also improved its clarity and maintainability.

Finally, we had to ensure numerical stability during the transition from NumPy. One source of instability was identified as differences in type promotion semantics between the two libraries. Stable computations were achieved by explicitly managing data types and taking care with operations that could lead to unintended type promotions. Techniques such as data type specification, careful handling of division and logarithms, and gradient clipping were used to avoid problems such as NaN's and unbounded values in training.

CHAPTER 2: PROFILING COMPUTATION AND DEVICE MEMORY

Overview

This chapter shifts the focus to the profiling of computation and the management of device memory when utilising Google JAX for machine learning tasks. The measurement of JAX function execution times enables the evaluation of computational efficiency and the informed decision-making necessary to enhance processing speed, particularly when dealing with data sets of a similar nature to that of Fashion-MNIST.

Monitoring GPU memory usage is also recommended in order to prevent out-of-memory errors and ensure optimal utilization of hardware resources. This section explores memory consumption patterns in order to ascertain their efficacy in managing computational workloads. This understanding is essential for scaling up models and handling larger datasets without compromising performance. Subsequently, we examine techniques for representing computation graphs in order to obtain a more profound comprehension of the underlying operations and data flow within JAX models. The visualization of these graphs facilitates a more comprehensive understanding of the dependencies and structure of computations, which is beneficial for debugging and optimization efforts. Another crucial topic addressed in this chapter is the optimization of batch sizes. The adjustment of batch sizes has the potential to result in notable enhancements in training efficiency and resource utilization.

Finally, the chapter introduces gradient checkpointing as a technique to reduce the memory footprint during the training of a model. By saving intermediate activations in a strategic manner and recomputing them during the backward pass, gradient checkpointing enables the training of deeper and more complex models without exceeding memory limitations.

Measuring Execution Time of JAX Functions

In the previous chapters, various JAX codes were developed to train a neural network on the Fashion-MNIST dataset. While JAX offers significant performance improvements over NumPy through just-in-time compilation and automatic differentiation, certain parts of the code may still contain bottlenecks that hinder optimal performance. Identifying these bottlenecks is crucial for optimizing the code to achieve faster execution times and more efficient resource utilization. The challenge lies in systematically measuring the execution time of JAX functions and pinpointing the sections of the code that require optimization.

To identify and optimize performance bottlenecks in JAX code, it is essential to utilize profiling tools that measure execution time and analyze computational efficiency. JAX provides built-in functions for timing, and Python offers profiling libraries such as **`timeit`**, **`cProfile`**, and **`line_profiler`** that can be employed to gather detailed performance metrics. By applying these tools to the neural network code developed previously, insights can be obtained regarding which functions or operations are consuming the greatest time and resources. This information allows for the implementation of targeted optimization efforts, which can enhance overall performance.

Identifying Functions to Profile

It is recommended to begin by reviewing the neural network code from the previously discussed recipes, with a particular focus on the key functions involved in training:

- **forward_pass(params, x)**: Computes the model's predictions.
- **compute_loss(params, x, y)**: Calculates the loss between predictions and true labels.
- **update(params, x, y)**: Updates model parameters using gradients.

These above functions are critical to the training loop and are prime candidates for profiling to assess their execution times.

Using JAX's Built-in Timing Function

There is a simple way to measure the execution time of a function using **jax.experimental.host_callback.timer**. However, a more straightforward approach is to use Python's **time** module for initial timing measurements.

```
import time

# Timing the forward_pass function

start_time = time.time()

y_pred = forward_pass(params, x_batch)

end_time = time.time()

print(f"Execution time of forward_pass: {end_time -
start_time} seconds")
```

This above method provides a basic understanding of how long the **forward_pass** function takes to execute with a given batch of data.

Profiling with 'timeit' and 'cProfile'

The **timeit** module offers more accurate timing by running the function multiple times and averaging the results.

```
import timeit
```

```
# Define a wrapper function for timeit

def time_forward_pass():

    y_pred = forward_pass(params, x_batch)

# Measure execution time

execution_time = timeit.timeit(time_forward_pass,
number=100) / 100

print(f"Average execution time of forward_pass:
{execution_time} seconds")
```

By executing the function repeatedly, **timeit** mitigates the effects of transient system load and provides a more reliable measurement.

For a more detailed analysis, the **cProfile** module can be used to profile the entire training loop.

```
import cProfile

import pstats

import io

pr = cProfile.Profile()

pr.enable()

# Training loop to profile

for epoch in range(num_epochs):

    # Training code as implemented previously

    pass

pr.disable()

s = io.StringIO()
```

```
ps = pstats.Stats(pr, stream=s).sort_stats('cumulative')
ps.print_stats()
# Display profiling results
print(s.getvalue())
```

The output will show a breakdown of function calls and the time spent in each, helping to identify which functions consume the most time during training.

Using 'line_profiler' for Line-by-Line Analysis

Here, to profile individual lines within a function, the **line_profiler** module can be employed. First, decorate the function to be profiled with **@profile**.

```
# Add this decorator to the function you want to profile
@profile
def forward_pass(params, x):
    # Function code
    pass
```

Run the above script using the **kernprof** command as shown below:

```
kernprof -l -v your_script.py
```

This above command generates a line-by-line profile report, indicating how much time is spent on each line within the function.

Profiling JIT-compiled Functions

Profiling JIT-compiled functions requires special consideration because JIT compilation itself takes time, and the first execution includes the compilation overhead. To obtain accurate measurements, run the function once to trigger compilation and then profile subsequent runs.

```
# Warm-up run to trigger JIT compilation
```

```
_ = update(params, x_batch, y_batch)

# Measure execution time excluding compilation overhead

start_time = time.time()

params = update(params, x_batch, y_batch)

end_time = time.time()

print(f"Execution time of update (post-compilation):
{end_time - start_time} seconds")
```

This approach ensures that the timing reflects the actual execution time without the initial compilation delay.

Monitoring GPU Memory Usage

While training the neural network on the Fashion-MNIST dataset using JAX, out-of-memory (OOM) errors may occur on the GPU. These errors interrupt the training process and are caused by the model consuming more memory than the GPU can provide. Managing GPU memory effectively is crucial for efficient model training, especially with large datasets or complex models. The challenge is to implement strategies to profile GPU memory usage and reduce consumption, ensuring that the model fits within the available memory constraints and training proceeds smoothly.

To address GPU OOM errors, it is essential to monitor and profile GPU memory usage during training. By understanding how memory is allocated and utilized, strategies can be implemented to reduce consumption. Techniques such as using smaller data types, optimizing data loading, adjusting batch sizes, and leveraging JAX's memory management features can help mitigate OOM errors. Below is a practical approach to profile and reduce GPU memory usage during model training with JAX.

Profiling GPU Memory Usage

The initial step is to monitor the GPU memory usage in order to identify the instances and locations where memory spikes occur. To gain insight into the real-time GPU memory consumption, one may utilize tools such as NVIDIA's nvidia-smi.

```
# Run this command in a separate terminal
```

```
watch -n 1 nvidia-smi
```

This command updates the GPU status every second, displaying memory usage and other statistics.

Preventing JAX from Preallocating GPU Memory

By default, JAX may preallocate the majority of the GPU memory, which can impede the ability to accurately monitor actual usage. To ensure precise profiling, it is necessary to disable preallocation.

```
import os

# Disable JAX GPU memory preallocation

os.environ['XLA_PYTHON_CLIENT_PREALLOCATE'] = 'false'
```

The setting of this environment variable guarantees that JAX will allocate memory as required, rather than reserving it in advance.

Reducing Data Precision

Utilising more compact data types can result in a reduction in memory consumption. It is recommended that data and model parameters be converted from float32 to float16.

```
import jax.numpy as jnp

from jax import random

# Convert data to float16

train_images = train_images.astype(jnp.float16)

test_images = test_images.astype(jnp.float16)

# Initialize parameters with float16

key = random.PRNGKey(0)

W1 = random.normal(key, (input_size, hidden_size),
dtype=jnp.float16) * 0.01
```

```
b1 = jnp.zeros((hidden_size,), dtype=jnp.float16)

W2 = random.normal(key, (hidden_size, output_size),
dtype=jnp.float16) * 0.01

b2 = jnp.zeros((output_size,), dtype=jnp.float16)
```

The use of **`float16`** halves the memory required for storing data and parameters.

Adjusting Batch Size

Reducing the batch size decreases the amount of data processed at once, thus lowering memory usage.

```
# Reduce batch size

batch_size = 32  # Previously 64
```

A smaller batch size requires less memory but may affect training dynamics. Try to find a balance between memory constraints and training efficiency.

Optimizing Data Loading

Here, ensure that data loading is efficient and does not consume unnecessary memory.

- Load data in batches rather than all at once.
- Use data generators or iterators to stream data during training.
- Avoid duplicating data in memory.

```
def data_generator(images, labels, batch_size):

    num_samples = images.shape[0]

    indices = jnp.arange(num_samples)

    for start_idx in range(0, num_samples, batch_size):

        excerpt = indices[start_idx:start_idx +
batch_size]
```

```
        yield images[excerpt], labels[excerpt]

# Use the generator in the training loop

for epoch in range(num_epochs):

    for x_batch, y_batch in data_generator(train_images,
train_labels, batch_size):

        params = update(params, x_batch, y_batch)
```

This whole approach loads only the necessary data into memory for each batch, conserving memory resources.

Utilizing JAX's 'jit' Compilation

Ensure that the **`@jit`** decorator is used appropriately to prevent excessive memory usage due to recompilation.

```
from jax import jit

# Use static_argnums if function arguments change shape
frequently

@jit

def update(params, x, y):

    grads = grad_loss(params, x, y)

    params = [param - learning_rate * grad for param,
grad in zip(params, grads)]

    return params
```

Where feasible, it is advisable to ensure that the input shapes remain consistent to circumvent the necessity for recompilation, which can otherwise result in the utilisation of additional memory.

Implementing Gradient Checkpointing

Gradient checkpointing trades computation for memory by re-computing parts of the forward pass during backpropagation instead of storing all intermediate activations.

```
from jax.experimental import checkpoint

# Apply checkpointing to the forward pass

def forward_pass(params, x):

    W1, b1, W2, b2 = params

    z1 = jnp.dot(x, W1) + b1

    a1 = relu(z1)

    z2 = jnp.dot(a1, W2) + b2

    return z2

# Use checkpointed version of the forward pass

checkpointed_forward = checkpoint(forward_pass)
```

By using **checkpoint**, memory usage during training is reduced at the cost of additional computation time.

Monitoring Memory Allocation with JAX Profiling Tools

Again you use JAX's profiling tools to get detailed information about memory allocation.

```
from jax import profiler

# Start profiling

profiler.start_trace('/tmp/jax_trace')

# Run training code

# Stop profiling

profiler.stop_trace()
```

you can also use TensorBoard to visualize the profiling data.

```
tensorboard --logdir=/tmp/jax_trace
```

Here, navigate to the "Profiler" tab to analyze memory usage and identify potential optimizations.

Minimizing Data Transfers between Host and Device

Excessive data transfers between the CPU (host) and GPU (device) can consume memory and reduce performance. Keep data on the device when possible.

```
from jax import device_put

# Move data to the GPU before training

train_images_device = device_put(train_images)

train_labels_device = device_put(train_labels)
```

Ensure that computations are performed on the GPU to avoid unnecessary data movement.

Simplifying Model Architecture

Consider reducing the complexity of the model to lower memory requirements.

- Decrease the number of neurons in hidden layers.
- Use shallower architectures.
- Employ model pruning techniques to remove redundant parameters.

```
# Reduce hidden layer size

hidden_size = 64  # Previously 128
```

A simpler model consumes less memory and may still achieve acceptable performance.

Utilizing Mixed Precision Training

One may leverage mixed precision training to achieve a balanced utilization of memory and computational efficiency.

```
from jax.experimental import mixed_precision
```

```
# Set policy for mixed precision

policy =
mixed_precision.Policy(compute_dtype=jnp.float16,
param_dtype=jnp.float32, output_dtype=jnp.float32)

mixed_precision.set_policy(policy)
```

Here, computations are performed in **float16**, reducing memory usage, while parameters are stored in **float32** for numerical stability.

Through the implementation of these strategies, it is possible to reduce the consumption of GPU memory effectively, which in turn serves to mitigate the occurrence of OOM (out of memory) errors that may occur during the process of model training. It is essential to profile and optimize memory usage when training models using JAX. This allows for the handling of larger datasets or more complex architectures, while still adhering to the constraints of available hardware resources.

Visualizing Computation Graphs

The development of complex neural network models with Google JAX can present a challenge when it comes to understanding the flow of computations. The complex layering and operational structure of these models makes it challenging to diagnose errors or enhance performance without a comprehensive understanding of the underlying computation graph. This lack of visibility impairs the ability to comprehend the manner in which data traverses the model and the nature of the interconnections between operations. The objective is to employ graph visualization tools that are compatible with JAX to examine and comprehend the computational graphs that are generated during the training of a model. This will facilitate the process of debugging and optimization.

Now, to visualize computation graphs in JAX, one effective approach is to integrate JAX with TensorBoard, a visualization tool that provides insights into machine learning models. While TensorBoard is traditionally used with TensorFlow, it can be employed with JAX by leveraging the **jax2tf** converter, which transforms JAX functions into TensorFlow operations.

Assuming that TensorFlow and TensorBoard are already installed (refer to Recipe 1 for installation steps), begin by importing the required libraries:

```
import jax

import jax.numpy as jnp
```

```
from jax import random
from jax.experimental import jax2tf
import tensorflow as tf
from tensorflow.summary import create_file_writer
```

Prepare Sample Data and Parameters

First, select a sample input from the training data and ensure model parameters are initialized:

```
# Sample input
x_sample = train_images[0:1]  # Using the first image as a sample
x_sample = x_sample.astype(jnp.float32)
# Initialize parameters (assuming parameters are already initialized)
params = [W1, b1, W2, b2]  # Replace with actual parameters
```

Convert JAX Functions to TensorFlow Functions

Then, use the **jax2tf.convert** function to convert the JAX **forward_pass** function to a TensorFlow-compatible function:

```
# Define the forward_pass function if not already defined
def forward_pass(params, x):
    W1, b1, W2, b2 = params
    z1 = jnp.dot(x, W1) + b1
    a1 = jnp.maximum(0, z1)  # ReLU activation
```

```
    z2 = jnp.dot(a1, W2) + b2

    return z2

# Convert to TensorFlow function

tf_forward_pass =
tf.function(jax2tf.convert(forward_pass))
```

Setup TensorBoard Logging

After this, create a log directory and a summary writer to record the computation graph:

```
logdir = 'logs/graph'

writer = create_file_writer(logdir)
```

Trace Computation Graph

Now within the summary writer context, execute the TensorFlow-converted function to capture the computation graph:

```
with writer.as_default():

    # Execute the function to trace the graph


tf.summary.graph(tf_forward_pass.get_concrete_function(pa
rams, x_sample))
```

Here, ensure that **params** and **x_sample** are compatible with TensorFlow functions. Convert them to TensorFlow tensors if necessary:

```
# Convert parameters and sample input to TensorFlow
tensors

params_tf = [tf.convert_to_tensor(p) for p in params]
```

```
x_sample_tf = tf.convert_to_tensor(x_sample)
```

Launch TensorBoard

After this, start TensorBoard to visualize the computation graph:

```
tensorboard --logdir=logs/graph
```

Open a web browser and navigate to **http://localhost:6006** to access the TensorBoard interface.

In TensorBoard, select the "Graphs" tab to view the computation graph generated from the model. The graph displays nodes representing operations and edges indicating the flow of data. Explore the graph to understand:

- The sequence of operations in the model.
- How data flows through layers.
- Dependencies between different computations.

This visualization helps identify any unnecessary complexity or potential optimization points within the model.

Enhance Graph Readability with Named Scopes

To improve the clarity of the computation graph, add named scopes to the model's functions. This groups related operations together, making the graph more organized:

```
def forward_pass(params, x):

    W1, b1, W2, b2 = params

    with tf.name_scope('Layer1'):

        z1 = jnp.dot(x, W1) + b1

        a1 = jnp.maximum(0, z1)

    with tf.name_scope('Layer2'):

        z2 = jnp.dot(a1, W2) + b2
```

```
    return z2
```

Re-run the steps to convert the function and trace the computation graph to see the updated, more readable graph in TensorBoard.

For a deeper understanding, inspect the JAXpr (JAX's intermediate representation) of the **forward_pass** function:

```
from jax import make_jaxpr

# Generate and print the JAXpr

jaxpr = make_jaxpr(forward_pass)(params, x_sample)

print(jaxpr)
```

The JAXpr provides a low-level view of the computations, showing primitive operations and how data flows between them. Try consider using additional tools like Netron or Graphviz for more advanced visualization.

The integration of JAX with TensorBoard and the utilisation of additional visualisation tools enables the effective inspection and comprehension of the computational graphs of complex models. This approach facilitates the debugging of issues, the optimization of performance, and a more profound comprehension of the operational mechanisms of the model.

Optimizing Batch Sizes for Performance

In the context of training neural networks using Google JAX, the selection of an optimal batch size is of paramount importance for the purpose of achieving efficient computation and effective memory utilization. An inadequate batch size has the potential to impede optimal training outcomes or, in extreme cases, precipitate out-of-memory (OOM) errors, particularly in instances where GPUs are constrained by their memory limitations. The objective is to identify a batch size that balances the computation time and memory usage in order to maximize training efficiency, while not exceeding the hardware limitations. It is imperative to profile different batch sizes in order to comprehend their impact on performance and to make well-informed decisions regarding the optimal batch size for a given training setup.

In order to determine the optimal batch size, it is necessary to profile the training process using various batch sizes and analyse their effects on both computation time and memory usage. By conducting a systematic experiment with varying batch sizes, one can observe the impact of these variables on training speed and resource consumption. The objective is to identify a batch size that provides an optimal balance between computational efficiency and memory requirements. This entails measuring the time required for each training epoch, monitoring the utilization of graphics processing unit (GPU) memory, and evaluating the overall performance of the model with each batch size.

Understanding Impact of Batch Size

Batch size refers to the number of training samples processed before the model's internal parameters are updated. Larger batch sizes can lead to faster computation per epoch due to the parallel processing capabilities of modern hardware like GPUs. However, larger batches consume more memory, which may not be available, leading to potential OOM errors. Smaller batch sizes reduce memory usage but may result in longer training times and less stable gradient estimates. It is important to find a balance that leverages hardware capabilities while staying within memory constraints.

Setting up Experiment

Begin by defining a range of batch sizes to test. Common batch sizes include powers of two, such as 16, 32, 64, 128, and 256. Prepare the training code to accept a variable batch size parameter so that the same codebase can be used for different batch sizes without modification.

```
# Define possible batch sizes to test

batch_sizes = [16, 32, 64, 128, 256]
```

Ensure that the data loading and training functions are designed to handle different batch sizes by accepting the batch size as an input parameter.

Modifying Data Loader

Adjust the data generator or data loader function to accept the batch size as an argument. Refer to the data generator implemented in Recipe 2 for efficient data loading.

```
def data_generator(images, labels, batch_size):

    num_samples = images.shape[0]

    indices = jnp.arange(num_samples)

    for start_idx in range(0, num_samples, batch_size):
```

```
        excerpt = indices[start_idx:start_idx +
batch_size]

        yield images[excerpt], labels[excerpt]
```

This function now allows for flexible batch sizes during training.

Implementing Timing and Memory Profiling

To measure computation time and memory usage, integrate timing functions and memory monitoring tools into the training loop. Use Python's **`time`** module to measure training time per epoch and **`nvidia-smi`** or JAX's built-in tools to monitor GPU memory usage.

```
import time

from jax.lib import xla_bridge

# Check if running on GPU

device = xla_bridge.get_backend().platform

print(f"Running on {device}")
```

Running Training Experiments with Different Batch Sizes

For each batch size in the defined range, perform the following steps:

- Initialize the model parameters.
- Train the model for a fixed number of epochs (e.g., one epoch for testing purposes).
- Measure the total training time.
- Monitor the peak GPU memory usage during training.

Following is the sample code for running the experiment with a specific batch size:

```
for batch_size in batch_sizes:

    print(f"\nTesting with batch size: {batch_size}")
```

```
    # Re-initialize model parameters

    params = initialize_params()


    # Record the start time

    start_time = time.time()


    # Training loop for one epoch

    for x_batch, y_batch in data_generator(train_images,
train_labels, batch_size):

        # Convert data to JAX arrays if necessary

        x_batch = jnp.array(x_batch)

        y_batch = jnp.array(y_batch)


        # Perform a training step

        params = update(params, x_batch, y_batch)


    # Record the end time

    end_time = time.time()


    # Calculate training time

    training_time = end_time - start_time
```

```
    print(f"Training time for batch size {batch_size}:
{training_time:.2f} seconds")


    # Monitor GPU memory usage (use nvidia-smi externally
or JAX profiling tools)

    print("GPU memory usage needs to be monitored
externally using nvidia-smi.")
```

Monitoring GPU Memory Usage

Since JAX does not provide direct methods to monitor GPU memory usage within the code, use the **nvidia-smi** command-line tool in a separate terminal to observe memory consumption during training.

```
watch -n 1 nvidia-smi
```

Here, do make a note of the peak memory usage for each batch size during the training process.

Recording and Analyzing Results

Here, collect the training time and peak memory usage data for each batch size tested. Organize the results in a table or spreadsheet for easy comparison.

Given below is an example:

Batch Size	Training Time (s)	Peak GPU Memory Usage (MiB)
16	120	2000
32	70	2500
64	40	4000

128	25	7000
256	Out of Memory	Exceeded GPU capacity

While larger batch sizes can speed up training, they may impact the quality of gradient estimation. Smaller batch sizes introduce more noise into the gradient calculation, which can sometimes help in escaping local minima but may also slow down convergence. It is important to monitor the model's performance metrics, such as training and validation accuracy, to ensure that the chosen batch size does not negatively affect learning.

Adjusting Learning Rate based on Batch Size

Consider adjusting the learning rate when changing the batch size. A common practice is to scale the learning rate proportionally with the batch size to maintain consistent gradient updates.

```
# Adjust learning rate

base_learning_rate = 0.01

adjusted_learning_rate = base_learning_rate * (batch_size / 64)  # Assuming 64 as the base batch size

# Use adjusted_learning_rate in the update function

def update(params, x, y, learning_rate):

    grads = grad_loss(params, x, y)

    params = [param - learning_rate * grad for param, grad in zip(params, grads)]

    return params
```

Try to include the adjusted learning rate in the training loop accordingly.

Implementing Gradient Accumulation

If hardware limitations prevent using larger batch sizes, implement gradient accumulation to simulate a larger effective batch size without increasing memory usage.

```
accumulation_steps = desired_batch_size //
actual_batch_size

accumulated_grads = None

step = 0

for x_batch, y_batch in data_generator(train_images,
train_labels, actual_batch_size):

    x_batch = jnp.array(x_batch)

    y_batch = jnp.array(y_batch)


    grads = grad_loss(params, x_batch, y_batch)


    if accumulated_grads is None:

        accumulated_grads = grads

    else:

        accumulated_grads = [ag + g for ag, g in
zip(accumulated_grads, grads)]


    step += 1

    if step % accumulation_steps == 0:

        # Update parameters with accumulated gradients

        params = [param - (learning_rate /
accumulation_steps) * ag for param, ag in zip(params,
accumulated_grads)]
```

```
        accumulated_grads = None
# Reset accumulated gradients
        step = 0
```

This approach allows for effective larger batch sizes while keeping per-step memory usage low.

This systematic approach allows for maximizing hardware utilization while avoiding OOM errors, ultimately leading to faster and more effective training of neural networks on the Fashion-MNIST dataset.

Reducing Memory Footprint with Gradient Checkpointing

When training a neural network on the Fashion-MNIST dataset using Google JAX, limited GPU memory can become a significant constraint. Large models or deep architectures require substantial memory to store activations during the forward pass, which can lead to OOM errors and hinder the training process. Reducing batch size might alleviate memory issues but can negatively impact training efficiency and convergence. The challenge is to find a way to train complex models within the available GPU memory without sacrificing performance. Applying gradient checkpointing methods allows us to trade additional computation for reduced memory usage, enabling the training of larger models on memory-constrained hardware.

Gradient checkpointing, also known as rematerialization, is a technique that reduces memory consumption during training by selectively storing and recomputing intermediate activations. Instead of keeping all activations in memory for backpropagation, certain activations are discarded after the forward pass and recomputed during the backward pass as needed. This approach lowers the memory footprint at the cost of increased computation time.

Understanding Forward Pass Structure

Begin by examining the **forward_pass** function used in the neural network:

```
def forward_pass(params, x):
    W1, b1, W2, b2 = params
    z1 = jnp.dot(x, W1) + b1
```

```
    a1 = jnp.maximum(0, z1)  # ReLU activation

    z2 = jnp.dot(a1, W2) + b2

    y_pred = jnp.exp(z2) / jnp.sum(jnp.exp(z2), axis=1,
keepdims=True)  # Softmax

    return y_pred
```

In the above function, activations **a1** and **z2** consume memory during training. For deep networks with many layers, the cumulative memory required to store all activations can exceed GPU capacity.

Applying 'jax.checkpoint' to Forward Pass

To implement gradient checkpointing, wrap parts of the forward pass with **jax.checkpoint** to indicate that intermediate values can be recomputed during the backward pass:

```
from jax import checkpoint

def forward_pass(params, x):

    W1, b1, W2, b2 = params

    # Define functions for each layer

    def layer1(x):

        return jnp.maximum(0, jnp.dot(x, W1) + b1)

    def layer2(a1):

        return jnp.dot(a1, W2) + b2

    # Apply checkpointing to layers

    a1 = checkpoint(layer1)(x)

    z2 = checkpoint(layer2)(a1)

    # Compute output
```

```
    y_pred = jnp.exp(z2) / jnp.sum(jnp.exp(z2), axis=1,
keepdims=True)

    return y_pred
```

By checkpointing **layer1** and **layer2**, intermediate activations **z1** and **a1** are not stored during the forward pass but are recomputed during backpropagation.

Adjusting Loss Function and Gradient Computation

It is essential to guarantee that the loss function and gradient computations are compatible with the checkpointed forward pass, as illustrated below:

```
def compute_loss(params, x, y):

    y_pred = forward_pass(params, x)

    loss = -
jnp.mean(jnp.log(y_pred[jnp.arange(y.shape[0]), y]))

    return loss

from jax import grad

grad_loss = grad(compute_loss)
```

Training Model with Checkpointing

Next, proceed with the training loop as before, using the same optimizer and update functions:

```
def update(params, x, y, learning_rate=0.01):

    grads = grad_loss(params, x, y)

    params = [p - learning_rate * g for p, g in
zip(params, grads)]

    return params

# Training loop
```

```
num_epochs = 10

batch_size = 64

for epoch in range(num_epochs):

    for x_batch, y_batch in data_generator(train_images,
train_labels, batch_size):

        x_batch = jnp.array(x_batch)

        y_batch = jnp.array(y_batch)

        params = update(params, x_batch, y_batch)
```

The use of **checkpoint** within the **forward_pass** function reduces memory consumption during training.

For models with more layers or complex architectures, consider applying checkpointing more selectively or using custom strategies:

Checkpointing Groups of Layers

In a deep network, grouping multiple layers and checkpointing the group can balance the trade-off between memory savings and computational overhead:

```
def forward_pass(params, x):

    activations = x

    for i in range(0, len(params), 2):  # Assuming pairs
of (W, b)

        W, b = params[i], params[i+1]

        def layer(a, W, b):

            return jnp.maximum(0, jnp.dot(a, W) + b)

        # Checkpoint the group of layers
```

```
        activations = checkpoint(layer)(activations, W,
b)

    return activations
```

Using 'jax.remat' with Custom Policies

For finer control, use **`jax.remat`** with a custom policy to specify which operations to checkpoint:

```
from jax import remat

def custom_policy(primitive):

    # Decide whether to checkpoint based on the primitive
name

    return primitive.name in ('dot_general',
'conv_general_dilated')

def forward_pass(params, x):

    remat_forward = remat(forward_pass_body,
policy=custom_policy)

    return remat_forward(params, x)
```

When using convolutional layers, memory consumption can be significant. You can apply checkpointing to convolutional layers as below:

```
def conv_layer(params, x):

    W, b = params

    return jax.nn.relu(jax.lax.conv_general_dilated(

        x, W, window_strides=(1, 1), padding='SAME'

    ) + b)
```

```
def forward_pass(params, x):
    # Apply checkpointing to convolutional layers
    x = checkpoint(conv_layer)(params[0], x)
    x = checkpoint(conv_layer)(params[1], x)
    # Continue with other layers
    return x
```

The incorporation of gradient checkpointing into the neural network training process enables the alleviation of memory constraints, thereby facilitating the training of larger or deeper models on GPUs with constrained memory resources. Although this approach necessitates additional computation due to the recomputation of activations, it offers a viable solution for surmounting hardware constraints.

Summary

We started by looking at ways to measure the execution time of JAX functions. By identifying the bottlenecks in the code, we were able to optimize performance using JAX's built-in tools and Python profiling libraries, including time, cProfile, and line_profiler. We implemented strategies to profile and reduce device memory consumption. We used smaller data types like float16 instead of float32, employed generators or iterators to optimize data loading, and adjusted batch sizes to balance memory usage and computational efficiency.

We addressed the issue of understanding the flow of complex computations in the model by utilizing graph visualization tools. This visualization helped us understand the data flow and dependencies within the model, allowing us to debug issues and optimize performance more effectively. Adding named scopes and analyzing the intermediate representation (JAXpr) provided deeper insights into the model's structure. Next, we must optimize batch sizes for training efficiency. Smaller batch sizes reduce memory consumption but increase training time due to less efficient hardware utilization. Larger batch sizes were shown to improve computational efficiency, but risked exceeding memory limitations. The chapter then explored how to reduce the memory footprint during training through the use of gradient checkpointing methods, which allow for the selective storing and recomputation of intermediate activations during the backward pass. This enabled the training of deeper and more complex models without exceeding memory constraints.

Overall, the chapter provided clear and practical techniques and strategies for profiling and optimizing both computation and memory usage when working with Google JAX.

CHAPTER 3: DEBUGGING RUNTIME VALUES AND ERRORS

Overview

In this chapter, we will tackle the challenges of debugging runtime values and errors head-on. We will equip you with practical strategies to identify and resolve common issues that may arise during model development and training. Once you understand the root causes of these errors, you can enhance the reliability and robustness of your machine learning models.

We'll start with concretization errors, which occur when JAX transformations encounter values that can't be determined at compile time. These errors can be subtle and will disrupt the flow of your program. You can write more flexible and efficient code by learning how to handle them effectively. Next, we'll tackle the challenge of inspecting intermediate values within JIT-compiled functions. Since traditional debugging methods like print statements may not work as expected, we introduce tools and techniques to examine the internal states of your computations. Dealing with shape mismatch errors is another common challenge, especially with complex neural network architectures. We provide practical solutions to diagnose and fix these errors, ensuring that your tensor operations align correctly.

Finally, we tackle issues related to NaNs appearing in computations, which can derail training and degrade model performance. You will learn how to understand the sources of numerical instability and implement appropriate remedies, maintaining the health of your models. By the end, you will have a comprehensive toolkit for debugging and resolving runtime errors in JAX, enabling you to develop more effective and reliable machine learning applications.

Handling Concretization Errors

When working with Google JAX to train neural networks, you may encounter a **`ConcretizationTypeError`** while using control flow constructs within JAX transformations like **`jit`**, **`grad`**, or **`vmap`**. This error occurs when JAX attempts to use a value during compilation that can only be determined at runtime. Such situations arise when control flow depends on data that isn't known until execution, conflicting with JAX's requirement for static computation graphs. The challenge is to understand why these errors occur and how to restructure your code to prevent them, ensuring smooth and efficient model training.

Understanding Concretization Errors

In JAX, functions transformed by **`jit`** (just-in-time compilation) or **`grad`** (automatic differentiation) are compiled into XLA (Accelerated Linear Algebra) computations. During this compilation, JAX traces the function to build a static computation graph. If the function includes control flow statements (like **`if`**, **`for`**, or **`while`**) that depend on runtime data, JAX cannot construct a static graph, leading to a **`ConcretizationTypeError`**. This error indicates that a traced (symbolic) value was used in a context that requires a concrete (numeric) value.

Let us consider a simple function that applies a threshold to an input:

```
import jax

import jax.numpy as jnp

@jax.jit

def threshold(x, threshold_value):

    if x > threshold_value:

        return x

    else:

        return 0.0

result = threshold(5.0, 3.0)
```

This code will raise a **ConcretizationTypeError** because the **if** statement depends on the value of **x**, which is a runtime variable. JAX cannot evaluate this condition during compilation since **x** is a symbolic placeholder at that stage.

To resolve concretization errors, you need to refactor your code to remove runtime-dependent control flow within JAX-transformed functions. JAX provides control flow primitives like **jax.lax.cond**, **jax.lax.switch**, and **jax.lax.scan** that handle dynamic control flow in a way compatible with JAX transformations.

Replace Python Control Flow with JAX Control Flow Primitives

Instead of using Python's **if** statements, use **jax.lax.cond** for conditional execution based on runtime values.

```
def threshold(x, threshold_value):

    return jax.lax.cond(

        x > threshold_value,

        lambda _: x,

        lambda _: 0.0,
```

```
        operand=None
    )
# JIT-compile the function
threshold_jit = jax.jit(threshold)
result = threshold_jit(5.0, 3.0)
```

Here, in this refactored code, **jax.lax.cond** allows the conditional logic to depend on runtime values within a JIT-compiled function.

Use Element-wise Operations for Arrays

If dealing with arrays, use element-wise operations provided by JAX, such as **jax.numpy.where**, to avoid control flow errors as shown below:

```
@jax.jit
def relu(x):
    return jnp.where(x > 0, x, 0.0)
# Apply to an array
x_array = jnp.array([-2.0, 0.0, 3.0])
result = relu(x_array)
```

This approach avoids using Python control flow and leverages JAX's optimized operations.

Handle Loops with 'jax.lax.scan' or 'jax.lax.fori_loop'

When loops depend on runtime values, replace them with JAX's looping constructs. Suppose you have a function that sums elements until a condition is met:

```
def cumulative_sum(x, max_value):
    total = 0.0
```

```
    for i in range(len(x)):
        total += x[i]
        if total > max_value:
            break
    return total
```

Refactor using **`jax.lax.fori_loop`**:

```
def cumulative_sum(x, max_value):
    def body_fun(i, val):
        total, done = val
        total += x[i] * (1 - done)
        done = jnp.where(total > max_value, 1.0, done)
        return total, done
    total, _ = jax.lax.fori_loop(
        0,
        len(x),
        body_fun,
        (0.0, 0.0)
    )
    return total
# JIT-compile the function
cumulative_sum_jit = jax.jit(cumulative_sum)
```

```
x_array = jnp.array([1.0, 2.0, 3.0, 4.0])

result = cumulative_sum_jit(x_array, 5.0)
```

Move Runtime-dependent Logic outside JIT Functions

If possible, handle control flow logic before calling JIT-compiled functions. Following is a quick example:

```
def adjust_learning_rate(epoch):

    if epoch < 5:

        return 0.01

    else:

        return 0.001

def train_step(params, x, y, learning_rate):

    grads = jax.grad(loss_fn)(params, x, y)

    new_params = [(p - learning_rate * g) for p, g in
zip(params, grads)]

    return new_params

# Training loop

for epoch in range(num_epochs):

    lr = adjust_learning_rate(epoch)

    params = jax.jit(train_step)(params, x_batch,
y_batch, lr)
```

By moving the learning rate adjustment outside the JIT-compiled **`train_step`** function, we avoid the concretization error.

Use Static Arguments with 'static_argnums'

If certain arguments need to be known at compile time, specify them as static arguments as shown below:

```
@jax.jit(static_argnums=(2,))

def train_step(params, x, y, training_phase):

    if training_phase == 'warmup':

        learning_rate = 0.01

    else:

        learning_rate = 0.001

    grads = jax.grad(loss_fn)(params, x, y)

    new_params = [(p - learning_rate * g) for p, g in
zip(params, grads)]

    return new_params

# Call the function with a static argument

params = train_step(params, x_batch, y_batch, 'warmup')
```

Here, be cautious with **`static_argnums`** as it can lead to recompilation if the static argument changes frequently.

An understanding of the cause of the **`ConcretizationTypeError`** and the application of appropriate restructuring techniques can prevent such errors and ensure the smooth running of JAX code. This approach enables the utilisation of JAX's robust transformations without compromising the flexibility required for dynamic control flow in machine learning models.

Inspecting Intermediate Values in JIT-Compiled Functions

When developing neural networks with Google JAX on the Fashion-MNIST dataset, debugging can become challenging, especially when functions are wrapped with **jit** for just-in-time compilation. Traditional debugging methods like inserting **print** statements do not work within **jit**-compiled functions because JAX traces the function to build a computation graph, and side-effecting operations like **print** are not executed during tracing. This makes it difficult to inspect intermediate values and understand the behavior of the code during execution. The challenge is to find effective methods to inspect runtime values within **jit**-compiled functions to facilitate debugging and ensure that the model functions correctly.

To overcome the difficulty of inspecting intermediate values in **jit**-compiled functions, we can utilize JAX's debugging tools, specifically **jax.debug.print**, which allows printing values during JAX transformations. Additionally, alternative methods like returning intermediate values or using host callbacks can be employed to inspect runtime values successfully. These techniques enable us to debug functions wrapped with **jit** and gain insights into the internal computations of our models.

Understanding Why 'print' Statements Fail?

Within **jit**-compiled functions, standard Python **print** statements are ignored because JAX operates by tracing functions to create static computation graphs. Side effects like **print** do not affect the computation graph and are therefore omitted during tracing.

Following is a quick example:

```
import jax

import jax.numpy as jnp

@jax.jit

def compute(x):

    y = x * 2

    print(f"Intermediate value y: {y}")

    return y

result = compute(3.0)
```

This code will not display the intermediate value of **y** because the **print** statement is not executed within the **jit**-compiled function.

Using 'jax.debug.print' for Debugging

Below is the refactored code using jax.debug.print

```
import jax

import jax.numpy as jnp

from jax import debug

@jax.jit

def compute(x):

    y = x * 2

    debug.print("Intermediate value y: {}", y)

    return y

result = compute(3.0)
```

When running this code, the output will be:

```
Intermediate value y: 6.0
```

Here, the **`debug.print`** function accepts a format string and variables to display. It operates correctly within **`jit`**-compiled functions, allowing us to inspect intermediate values.

Applying 'jax.debug.print' in Model

Suppose we want to inspect intermediate activations within the neural network's forward pass. Following is a quick example:

```
def forward_pass(params, x):

    W1, b1, W2, b2 = params

    z1 = jnp.dot(x, W1) + b1

    a1 = jnp.maximum(0, z1)  # ReLU activation
```

```
    debug.print("Activation a1 mean: {}", jnp.mean(a1))

    z2 = jnp.dot(a1, W2) + b2

    y_pred = jax.nn.softmax(z2)

    return y_pred

forward_pass_jit = jax.jit(forward_pass)
```

By running **`forward_pass_jit(params, x_batch)`**, we can observe the mean value of **`a1`** during execution.

Conditional Debugging

We can add conditions to the **`debug.print`** function to limit output to specific cases. Following is a quick example:

```
def forward_pass(params, x):

    W1, b1, W2, b2 = params

    z1 = jnp.dot(x, W1) + b1

    a1 = jnp.maximum(0, z1)

    max_a1 = jnp.max(a1)

    debug.print("Max of a1: {}", max_a1, where=max_a1 >
10.0)

    z2 = jnp.dot(a1, W2) + b2

    y_pred = jax.nn.softmax(z2)

    return y_pred
```

This will print the maximum value of **`a1`** only when it exceeds **`10.0`**, helping to identify abnormal activations.

Using Host Callbacks with 'jax.experimental.host_callback'

For more advanced debugging, **jax.experimental.host_callback.id_print** can be used. Following is a quick example:

```
from jax.experimental import host_callback as hcb

@jax.jit

def compute(x):

    y = x * 2

    hcb.id_print(y, result=False, what="Intermediate
value y")

    return y

result = compute(3.0)
```

This method sends the value from the device to the host and prints it, providing a way to inspect values during execution.

By utilizing **jax.debug.print**, host callbacks, and alternative methods like returning intermediate values, we can effectively inspect runtime values within **jit**-compiled functions. These techniques enhance our ability to debug and understand the internal computations of our models.

Dealing with Shape Mismatch Errors

During matrix operations in neural networks trained with Google JAX, shape mismatch errors may arise, according to recent findings. Such errors emerge when the dimensions of tensors are not aligned correctly for the intended mathematical operations, including matrix multiplication and broadcasting. Shape mismatch errors are a common occurrence in machine learning workflows and can prove to be a significant challenge when attempting to identify the source and implement a solution, particularly in the context of complex models comprising multiple layers and data transformations. The objective is to implement verification and alignment strategies for tensor shapes prior to performing operations, thereby ensuring that the code functions without encountering shape-related errors.

To avoid shape mismatch errors, it is crucial to comprehend the anticipated dimensions of tensors throughout the computational process and to ascertain that these shapes are aligned correctly for the intended operations. This necessitates a meticulous examination of the shapes of the input data, the dimensions of the parameters, and the shapes of the outputs of each layer or function. By implementing systematic checks and utilizing JAX's debugging tools, shape inconsistencies can be identified and corrected before they result in runtime errors. The following section outlines practical strategies for verifying and aligning the shapes of tensors in JAX code.

Understanding Tensor Shapes in Model

Begin by reviewing the structure of your neural network and the expected shapes of tensors at each layer. For the Fashion-MNIST dataset, images are typically of shape **`(batch_size, 28, 28)`** for grayscale images. When flattening images for a fully connected network, the shape becomes **`(batch_size, 784)`**.

Following is a quick example:

```
# Assuming batch_size is 64

x_batch = jnp.array([...])  # Shape: (64, 28, 28)

y_batch = jnp.array([...])  # Shape: (64,)

# Flatten the input images

x_batch = x_batch.reshape(64, 784)  # Shape: (64, 784)
```

Verifying Parameter Shapes

The initialisation of model parameters should be performed using shapes that correspond to the expected dimensions for matrix operations. Following is the example of initializing weights and biases:

```
input_size = 784   # Number of input features

hidden_size = 128  # Number of neurons in the hidden
layer

output_size = 10   # Number of classes

key = random.PRNGKey(0)

W1 = random.normal(key, (input_size, hidden_size)) * 0.01
# Shape: (784, 128)
```

```
b1 = jnp.zeros((hidden_size,))  # Shape: (128,)

W2 = random.normal(key, (hidden_size, output_size)) *
0.01  # Shape: (128, 10)

b2 = jnp.zeros((output_size,))  # Shape: (10,)
```

It is advisable to ensure that weight matrices and bias vectors have shapes that are compatible with the operations performed in the forward pass.

Implementing Forward Pass with Shape Checks

When defining the forward pass, include shape checks or print statements to verify tensor dimensions. Following is a quick example of forward pass function:

```
def forward_pass(params, x):

    W1, b1, W2, b2 = params

    # First layer

    z1 = jnp.dot(x, W1) + b1  # x shape: (batch_size,
784), W1 shape: (784, 128)

    a1 = jax.nn.relu(z1)      # z1 shape: (batch_size,
128)

    # Second layer

    z2 = jnp.dot(a1, W2) + b2  # a1 shape: (batch_size,
128), W2 shape: (128, 10)

    y_pred = jax.nn.softmax(z2)  # z2 shape: (batch_size,
10)

    return y_pred
```

Here, you can include shape assertions to verify that the shapes are as expected:

```
def forward_pass(params, x):
```

```
    W1, b1, W2, b2 = params

    assert x.shape[1] == W1.shape[0], f"Shape mismatch: x
{x.shape}, W1 {W1.shape}"

    z1 = jnp.dot(x, W1) + b1

    assert z1.shape[1] == b1.shape[0], f"Shape mismatch:
z1 {z1.shape}, b1 {b1.shape}"

    a1 = jax.nn.relu(z1)

    assert a1.shape[1] == W2.shape[0], f"Shape mismatch:
a1 {a1.shape}, W2 {W2.shape}"

    z2 = jnp.dot(a1, W2) + b2

    assert z2.shape[1] == b2.shape[0], f"Shape mismatch:
z2 {z2.shape}, b2 {b2.shape}"

    y_pred = jax.nn.softmax(z2)

    return y_pred
```

IF you can include these assertions, it can help catch shape mismatches early in the computation.

Utilizing 'jax.debug.print' for Shape Inspection

Use **`jax.debug.print`** to print tensor shapes within JIT-compiled functions.

```
def forward_pass(params, x):

    W1, b1, W2, b2 = params

    z1 = jnp.dot(x, W1) + b1

    jax.debug.print("z1 shape: {}", z1.shape)

    a1 = jax.nn.relu(z1)
```

```
    jax.debug.print("a1 shape: {}", a1.shape)

    z2 = jnp.dot(a1, W2) + b2

    jax.debug.print("z2 shape: {}", z2.shape)

    y_pred = jax.nn.softmax(z2)

    jax.debug.print("y_pred shape: {}", y_pred.shape)

    return y_pred
```

This allows you to inspect the shapes during execution and identify any discrepancies.

Checking Input Data Shapes before Training

After this, before entering the training loop, try to verify the shapes of the input data.

```
print(f"x_batch shape: {x_batch.shape}")  # Should be
(batch_size, 784)

print(f"y_batch shape: {y_batch.shape}")  # Should be
(batch_size,)
```

With this, you ensure that the batch size and feature dimensions are correct.

Handling Broadcasting Issues

Now, when adding biases or performing element-wise operations, be mindful of broadcasting rules. For example, if **`b1`** has shape **`(128,)`** and **`z1`** has shape **`(batch_size, 128)`**, adding them works due to broadcasting. However, if **`b1`** has an incorrect shape, it may cause a shape mismatch.

With the following script, you ensure that biases are correctly shaped:

```
# Correct bias shapes

b1 = jnp.zeros((1, hidden_size))  # Shape: (1, 128)

b2 = jnp.zeros((1, output_size))  # Shape: (1, 10)
```

Then, adjust the forward pass accordingly:

```
z1 = jnp.dot(x, W1) + b1  # Shapes: (batch_size, 128) +
(1, 128)
```

Using Explicit Reshaping and Transposing

When necessary, use **jnp.reshape** and **jnp.transpose** to adjust tensor shapes.

Following is a quick example:

```
# If x has shape (batch_size, 28, 28), flatten it

x_flat = x.reshape(batch_size, -1)  # Now shape is
(batch_size, 784)
```

If you need to transpose a matrix:

```
W1_T = jnp.transpose(W1)  # Switches axes
```

We need to check that the reshaping and transposing operations align the tensors properly for subsequent operations.

Testing with Small Batches

Run tests with small batches of data to verify that shapes are correct before scaling up.

```
test_x = jnp.ones((2, 784))  # Small batch of size 2

test_params = [W1, b1, W2, b2]

test_output = forward_pass(test_params, test_x)

print(f"Test output shape: {test_output.shape}")  #
Should be (2, 10)
```

When a shape mismatch error occurs, JAX provides detailed error messages indicating the expected and actual shapes.

```
ValueError: Incompatible shapes for dot operation: lhs
shape (64, 784), rhs shape (129, 10)
```

After this, you can use this information to trace back to where the shapes diverged from expectations.

By implementing these strategies to verify and align tensor shapes before performing operations, you can prevent shape mismatch errors in your JAX code. It is of the utmost importance to exercise meticulous attention to the dimensions of tensors, to utilise assertions and debugging tools, and to undertake a systematic examination of shapes at each stage of the computation.

Resolving Issues with NaNs in Computations

When training a neural network on the Fashion-MNIST dataset using Google JAX, you may encounter situations where the model outputs **`NaN`** values during computations. These **`NaN`**s can propagate through the network, causing the training process to fail or produce invalid results. Numerical instability often leads to such issues, stemming from operations like division by zero, taking logarithms of zero, or exponential functions causing overflow. The challenge is to identify the sources of these **`NaN`**s and implement strategies to prevent them, ensuring stable and successful training.

To resolve issues with **`NaN`**s in computations, it's essential to pinpoint where they originate and address the underlying numerical instability. Some of the strategies that can be put intp use are:

- **Identifying and handling unstable operations**: Modify functions prone to numerical issues, like softmax or logarithms.
- **Applying regularization techniques**: Prevent weights from growing too large by using L2 regularization or dropout.
- **Implementing gradient clipping**: Limit the magnitude of gradients to prevent extreme updates.
- **Adjusting the learning rate**: Lower it if it's causing divergence.
- **Proper weight initialization**: Use methods like Xavier initialization to start with reasonable weight values.
- **Monitoring activations and gradients**: Inspect values during training to detect anomalies early.

Following is a step-by-step practical walkthrough to identify and resolve **`NaN`**s in your model.

Identifying Source of NaNs

First, determine where in the computation the **NaN**s are introduced. Modify your code to print intermediate values or use debugging tools.

```
for epoch in range(num_epochs):

    for x_batch, y_batch in data_generator(train_images,
train_labels, batch_size):

        x_batch = jnp.array(x_batch)

        y_batch = jnp.array(y_batch)

        params = update(params, x_batch, y_batch)

    # Compute loss on training data

    loss_value = compute_loss(params, x_batch, y_batch)

    print(f"Epoch {epoch}, Loss: {loss_value}")
```

If **loss_value** becomes **NaN**, it's an indication that **NaN**s have been introduced during the computation.

Checking for NaNs in Activations and Gradients

Use **jax.debug.print** to inspect intermediate values within **jit**-compiled functions.

```
from jax import debug

def forward_pass(params, x):

    W1, b1, W2, b2 = params

    z1 = jnp.dot(x, W1) + b1

    a1 = jax.nn.relu(z1)

    debug.print("Max of a1: {}", jnp.max(a1))

    z2 = jnp.dot(a1, W2) + b2
```

```
    y_pred = jax.nn.softmax(z2)
    debug.print("Max of y_pred: {}", jnp.max(y_pred))
    return y_pred
```

This helps identify if activations or outputs contain **NaN**s.

Handling Numerical Instability in Softmax Function

The softmax function can produce **NaN**s if exponentials overflow. Here, you can use a stable softmax implementation.

```
def stable_softmax(z):
    z_max = jnp.max(z, axis=1, keepdims=True)
    exp_z = jnp.exp(z - z_max)
    sum_exp_z = jnp.sum(exp_z, axis=1, keepdims=True)
    return exp_z / sum_exp_z
# Replace in forward_pass
y_pred = stable_softmax(z2)
```

Applying Gradient Clipping

Let us now limit the gradients' magnitude to prevent large updates that can cause instability.

```
from jax import tree_util
def clip_grads(grads, max_norm):
    total_norm = jnp.sqrt(sum([jnp.sum(jnp.square(g)) for
g in tree_util.tree_leaves(grads)]))
    clip_coef = jnp.minimum(1.0, max_norm / (total_norm +
1e-6))
```

```
    return tree_util.tree_map(lambda g: g * clip_coef,
grads)

def update(params, x, y, learning_rate=0.01):

    grads = grad_loss(params, x, y)

    grads = clip_grads(grads, max_norm=5.0)

    params = [p - learning_rate * g for p, g in
zip(params, grads)]

    return params
```

Adding Regularization

The regularization process serves to prevent the weights from becoming excessively large, thereby reducing the likelihood of encountering numerical issues.

```
def compute_loss(params, x, y, lambda_reg=0.001):

    y_pred = forward_pass(params, x)

    epsilon = 1e-7

    y_pred = jnp.clip(y_pred, epsilon, 1.0 - epsilon)

    log_probs = -jnp.log(y_pred[jnp.arange(y.shape[0]),
y])

    loss = jnp.mean(log_probs)

    # L2 regularization

    l2_loss = sum([jnp.sum(jnp.square(p)) for p in
params])

    total_loss = loss + lambda_reg * l2_loss

    return total_loss
```

In the above, a high learning rate can cause divergence. We can simply reduce it to stabilize training as below:

```
learning_rate = 0.001  # Reduced from 0.01
```

Proper Weight Initialization

We can also use methods like Xavier (Glorot) initialization to start with appropriate weight scales.

```
def glorot_init(key, shape):

    fan_in, fan_out = shape[0], shape[1]

    limit = jnp.sqrt(6 / (fan_in + fan_out))

    return random.uniform(key, shape, minval=-limit,
maxval=limit)

# Initialize weights

key = random.PRNGKey(0)

W1 = glorot_init(key, (input_size, hidden_size))

b1 = jnp.zeros((hidden_size,))

W2 = glorot_init(key, (hidden_size, output_size))

b2 = jnp.zeros((output_size,))
```

Using Alternative Activation Functions

There are possibilities where we can consider using activations less prone to causing **NaN**s, like Leaky ReLU as shown below:

```
def leaky_relu(x, alpha=0.01):

    return jnp.where(x > 0, x, alpha * x)

# Use in forward_pass
```

```
a1 = leaky_relu(z1)
```

We can then normalize the input data to prevent large activations.

```
mean = jnp.mean(train_images, axis=0)

std = jnp.std(train_images, axis=0) + 1e-7  # Prevent
division by zero

def normalize(x):

    return (x - mean) / std

# Normalize training data

train_images = normalize(train_images)
```

Implementing Batch Normalization

Batch normalization stabilizes activations across layers.

```
def batch_norm(x, gamma, beta, eps=1e-5):

    mean = jnp.mean(x, axis=0, keepdims=True)

    variance = jnp.var(x, axis=0, keepdims=True)

    x_norm = (x - mean) / jnp.sqrt(variance + eps)

    return gamma * x_norm + beta

# Initialize gamma and beta

gamma1 = jnp.ones((hidden_size,))

beta1 = jnp.zeros((hidden_size,))

# Include in params

params = [W1, b1, gamma1, beta1, W2, b2]
```

```
def forward_pass(params, x):
    W1, b1, gamma1, beta1, W2, b2 = params
    z1 = jnp.dot(x, W1) + b1
    z1_bn = batch_norm(z1, gamma1, beta1)
    a1 = jax.nn.relu(z1_bn)
    z2 = jnp.dot(a1, W2) + b2
    y_pred = stable_softmax(z2)
    return y_pred
```

Do not forget to use consistent data types to prevent precision-related **NaN**s.

```
x_batch = x_batch.astype(jnp.float32)
params = [p.astype(jnp.float32) for p in params]
```

By identifying sources of numerical instability and applying techniques like regularization, gradient clipping, proper initialization, and stable function implementations, you can resolve **NaN** issues in your computations.

Summary

In conclusion, this chapter provided solutions to overcome common runtime errors and debugging challenges encountered when using Google JAX for machine learning tasks. The chapter addressed concretization errors that arose when control flow in JAX transformations depended on runtime values. JAX requires static computation graphs, so we implemented strategies to restructure code using JAX's control flow primitives like jax.lax.cond and jax.lax.scan. Another crucial issue addressed was the challenge of inspecting intermediate values within JIT-compiled functions. We also examined shape mismatch errors, which often occurred during matrix operations. You can resolve this by checking the shapes of your input data, ensuring your parameter dimensions match the expected values, and using assertions or debug prints to confirm the shapes of your tensors at each computation step.

Finally, the chapter addressed the issue of NaN values appearing in computations, which can cause training failures. We identified the sources of numerical instability, such as operations prone to overflow or division by zero. Solutions implemented included applying regularization techniques to prevent weights from becoming excessively large, implementing gradient clipping to limit the magnitude of updates, adjusting learning rates, and using stable versions of mathematical functions like softmax. In summary, by understanding the causes of concretization errors, utilizing JAX-specific debugging tools, verifying tensor shapes, and addressing numerical instabilities, developers enhanced the reliability and robustness of their machine learning models on the Fashion-MNIST dataset.

CHAPTER 4: MASTERING PYTREES FOR DATA STRUCTURES

Overview

Pytrees are trees of Python containers like lists, tuples, and dictionaries. They are the ideal tool for representing complex hierarchical structures. This chapter will show you how Pytrees, an indispensable data structure in JAX, allows you to work flexibly with nested data.

We start by looking at the best ways to work with nested data using Pytrees. We'll show you the most practical methods for navigating and modifying these structures. It is essential to understand these operations if you want to handle parameters and configurations in machine learning models. Next, we show you how to create custom Pytrees for user-defined classes, enabling you to seamlessly integrate your own data types into JAX's ecosystem.

Finally, the chapter covers serializing and deserializing Pytrees, which is essential for saving and loading models or checkpoints. You will learn how to store Pytrees efficiently and reconstruct them later, ensuring that your models can be persisted without loss. Additionally, we discuss methods for filtering Pytrees to extract specific parameters or subsets of data, which you will find useful when applying different operations to parts of your model.

Manipulating Nested Data with Pytrees

When working with machine learning models involving complex architectures or large parameter sets, you often encounter deeply nested data structures. These structures can be composed of lists, tuples, dictionaries, and other containers holding arrays or scalars. Managing and manipulating such nested data becomes challenging when you need to apply transformations or operations uniformly across all elements. The difficulty intensifies when integrating these operations with JAX transformations like **`jit`**, **`grad`**, or **`vmap`**, which expect data in a specific format.

JAX introduces the concept of Pytrees, which are flexible, nested data structures composed of containers like lists, tuples, and dictionaries, with arrays or scalars as leaves. Pytrees allow you to represent complex hierarchical data in a way that JAX can understand and manipulate efficiently. JAX provides utility functions such as **`jax.tree_map`**, **`jax.tree_flatten`**, and **`jax.tree_unflatten`** to traverse and operate on Pytrees. By leveraging these tools, you can apply functions over nested structures without manually handling each level of nesting.

Understanding Pytrees

A PyTree is any nested structure of Python containers where the leaves are arrays or scalars. JAX treats these structures as trees, enabling operations over them.

Following is an example of a PyTree:

```
import jax
```

```
import jax.numpy as jnp

# Define a PyTree of model parameters

params = {

    'layer1': {

        'weights': jnp.array([[0.1, 0.2], [0.3, 0.4]]),

        'biases': jnp.array([0.1, 0.2])

    },

    'layer2': {

        'weights': jnp.array([[0.5, 0.6], [0.7, 0.8]]),

        'biases': jnp.array([0.3, 0.4])

    }

}
```

In this example, **params** is a nested dictionary containing JAX arrays as leaves.

Using 'jax.tree_map' to apply Functions over Pytrees

The **jax.tree_map** function applies a given function to each leaf in the PyTree, maintaining the overall structure.

See the below example of scaling all parameters:

```
# Function to scale parameters

def scale_fn(param):

    return param * 0.5

# Apply the scaling function over the PyTree
```

```
scaled_params = jax.tree_map(scale_fn, params)
```

Here, **scaled_params** has the same structure as **params**, but each numerical value is halved.

Working with Multiple Pytrees

jax.tree_map can operate on multiple Pytrees simultaneously if they share the same structure. Given below is a demonstration of adding two Pytrees:

```
# Define another PyTree with the same structure

params2 = {

    'layer1': {

        'weights': jnp.array([[0.01, 0.02], [0.03,
0.04]]),

        'biases': jnp.array([0.01, 0.02])

    },

    'layer2': {

        'weights': jnp.array([[0.05, 0.06], [0.07,
0.08]]),

        'biases': jnp.array([0.03, 0.04])

    }

}

# Function to add parameters from two Pytrees

def add_fn(p1, p2):

    return p1 + p2

# Add corresponding leaves
```

```
sum_params = jax.tree_map(add_fn, params, params2)
```

Flattening and Unflattening Pytrees

We can use **jax.tree_flatten** to convert a PyTree into a flat list of leaves and a structure (treedef). Given below is a quick example of flattening a PyTree:

```
# Flatten the PyTree

leaves, treedef = jax.tree_flatten(params)

print("Leaves:", leaves)

print("TreeDef:", treedef)
```

We can unflattening the PyTree as below:

```
# Reconstruct the PyTree from leaves and treedef

reconstructed_params = jax.tree_unflatten(treedef,
leaves)
```

Applying JAX Transformations with Pytrees

Now, the JAX transformations like **grad** and **jit** work seamlessly with functions that accept Pytrees.

```
# Define a simple model function

def model(params, x):

    # Forward pass using parameters in PyTree

    a = x @ params['layer1']['weights'] +
params['layer1']['biases']

    a = jax.nn.relu(a)
```

```
    y = a @ params['layer2']['weights'] +
params['layer2']['biases']

    return y

# Define a loss function

def loss_fn(params, x, y_true):

    y_pred = model(params, x)

    loss = jnp.mean((y_pred - y_true) ** 2)

    return loss

# Generate some dummy data

x_data = jnp.array([[1.0, 2.0], [3.0, 4.0]])

y_data = jnp.array([[1.0, 2.0], [3.0, 4.0]])

# Compute gradients with respect to parameters

grads = jax.grad(loss_fn)(params, x_data, y_data)
```

Updating Parameters using Gradients

We can use **jax.tree_map** to update parameters based on gradients.

```
learning_rate = 0.01

# Function to update parameters

def update_fn(param, grad):

    return param - learning_rate * grad

# Update parameters

updated_params = jax.tree_map(update_fn, params, grads)
```

These Pytrees can contain any combination of nested containers. Below you can see nested lists and tuples:

```
# Define a more complex PyTree

complex_params = [

    {'weights': jnp.array([1.0, 2.0]), 'biases':
jnp.array([0.1, 0.2])},

    (

        {'weights': jnp.array([3.0, 4.0]), 'biases':
jnp.array([0.3, 0.4])},

        {'weights': jnp.array([5.0, 6.0]), 'biases':
jnp.array([0.5, 0.6])}

    )

]

# Apply a function over the complex PyTree

scaled_complex_params = jax.tree_map(lambda x: x * 2,
complex_params)
```

Filtering Leaves based on Conditions

You can then filter and operate on specific leaves using custom functions as below:

```
def is_weight(key, _):

    return key == 'weights'

def conditional_scale(tree):

    def scale_if_weight(key, val):

        if key == 'weights':
```

```
            return val * 0.5

        else:

            return val

    return jax.tree_map(scale_if_weight, tree,
is_leaf=lambda x: isinstance(x, dict))

scaled_params = conditional_scale(params)
```

Define Custom PyTree Nodes

You can also define custom objects as PyTree nodes by registering them with JAX. For example, you can register a custom class.

```
from jax import tree_util

class LayerParams:

    def __init__(self, weights, biases):

        self.weights = weights

        self.biases = biases

# Register LayerParams as a PyTree node

def layerparams_flatten(obj):

    children = (obj.weights, obj.biases)

    aux_data = None

    return children, aux_data

def layerparams_unflatten(aux_data, children):

    return LayerParams(*children)
```

```
tree_util.register_pytree_node(LayerParams,
layerparams_flatten, layerparams_unflatten)

# Use LayerParams in a PyTree

params_custom = {

    'layer1': LayerParams(weights=jnp.array([0.1]),
biases=jnp.array([0.2]))

}

# Apply a function over the PyTree

scaled_params_custom = jax.tree_map(lambda x: x * 2,
params_custom)
```

Later, integrate the Pytrees into your training loop for managing parameters and updates.

```
# Define the training loop

def train_step(params, x, y):

    grads = jax.grad(loss_fn)(params, x, y)

    params = jax.tree_map(lambda p, g: p - learning_rate
* g, params, grads)

    return params

# JIT-compile the training step

train_step_jit = jax.jit(train_step)

# Simulate training

for epoch in range(10):

    params = train_step_jit(params, x_data, y_data)
```

```
    current_loss = loss_fn(params, x_data, y_data)

    print(f"Epoch {epoch}, Loss: {current_loss}")
```

This whole approach enhances code maintainability and integrates seamlessly with JAX transformations, allowing for efficient computation and gradient calculations. Leveraging Pytrees empowers you to build and manage sophisticated machine learning models with ease.

Custom Pytrees for User-defined Classes

When building complex machine learning models with JAX, you might define custom classes to represent layers, modules, or other components. However, these user-defined classes are not automatically recognized by JAX's PyTree system. As a result, functions like **jax.tree_map**, **jax.tree_flatten**, and transformations such as **jit** or **grad** cannot traverse or manipulate the data within these custom objects. This incompatibility makes it difficult to integrate your custom classes with JAX's functionalities, hindering the seamless development of your models. The challenge is to make your custom classes compatible with JAX's Pytrees so that you can leverage JAX's powerful tools while maintaining clean and modular code.

To integrate custom classes with JAX's PyTree system, you can register your classes as PyTree nodes. This involves defining how your class can be flattened into its constituent leaves (the data it holds) and how it can be reconstructed (unflattened) from these leaves. By registering your class with JAX's **tree_util** module, you enable JAX to recognize and traverse instances of your class during transformations and when using PyTree utilities. This process allows your custom objects to be manipulated just like built-in container types, making them compatible with JAX functions.

Define Custom Class

Let us consider that we have a custom class representing a neural network layer:

```
import jax

import jax.numpy as jnp

class NeuralLayer:

    def __init__(self, weights, biases):

        self.weights = weights
```

```
        self.biases = biases

    def __call__(self, x):

        z = jnp.dot(x, self.weights) + self.biases

        return jax.nn.relu(z)
```

In this class, **weights** and **biases** are JAX arrays representing the parameters of the layer.

Use JAX Functions

Now, try using **jax.tree_map** on an instance of your class:

```
layer = NeuralLayer(weights=jnp.array([[0.1, 0.2], [0.3,
0.4]]),

                    biases=jnp.array([0.1, 0.2]))

# Attempt to scale the parameters

scaled_layer = jax.tree_map(lambda x: x * 0.5, layer)
```

This will raise an error because JAX does not know how to traverse **NeuralLayer**.

Next, define flattening and unflattening functions as learned previously.

```
from jax import tree_util

def neural_layer_flatten(layer):

    # The leaves are the parameters we want to transform

    leaves = (layer.weights, layer.biases)

    # Auxiliary data includes any static information
needed to reconstruct the object

    aux_data = {}

    return leaves, aux_data
```

```
def neural_layer_unflatten(aux_data, leaves):
    # Reconstruct the NeuralLayer object from leaves
    return NeuralLayer(*leaves)
```

Register Custom Class as a PyTree Node

Use **tree_util.register_pytree_node** to register your class:

```
tree_util.register_pytree_node(NeuralLayer,
                               neural_layer_flatten,
                               neural_layer_unflatten)
```

Then, you can use **jax.tree_map** and other JAX utilities with instances of your class:

```
# Scale the parameters of the layer
scaled_layer = jax.tree_map(lambda x: x * 0.5, layer)
# Verify the parameters have been scaled
print("Scaled Weights:\n", scaled_layer.weights)
print("Scaled Biases:\n", scaled_layer.biases)
```

Integrate with JAX Transformations

You can now include your custom class in functions that will be transformed by JAX, such as **jit** or **grad**. See the following wherein we are using jit with a custom layer:

```
# Define a function that uses the custom layer
def forward_pass(layer, x):
    return layer(x)
# JIT-compile the forward pass
```

```
forward_pass_jit = jax.jit(forward_pass)

# Test the JIT-compiled function

x_input = jnp.array([[1.0, 2.0]])

output = forward_pass_jit(layer, x_input)

print("Output:", output)
```

Compute Gradients

Now, compute gradients of a loss function with respect to the parameters in your custom class.

```
# Define a simple loss function

def loss_fn(layer, x, y_true):

    y_pred = layer(x)

    loss = jnp.mean((y_pred - y_true) ** 2)

    return loss

# Generate dummy data

x_data = jnp.array([[1.0, 2.0], [3.0, 4.0]])

y_data = jnp.array([[0.5, 1.0], [1.5, 2.0]])

# Compute gradients

grads = jax.grad(loss_fn)(layer, x_data, y_data)
```

Then, use **`jax.tree_map`** to apply parameter updates:

```
learning_rate = 0.01

# Update function

def update_params(param, grad):
```

```
    return param - learning_rate * grad

# Update the layer's parameters

updated_layer = jax.tree_map(update_params, layer, grads)
```

Combine Multiple Layers into a Model

You can compose multiple custom layers into a larger model:

```
class NeuralNetwork:

    def __init__(self, layers):

        self.layers = layers

    def __call__(self, x):

        for layer in self.layers:

            x = layer(x)

        return x

# Create multiple layers

layer1 = NeuralLayer(weights=jnp.array([[0.1, 0.2], [0.3,
0.4]]),

                     biases=jnp.array([0.1, 0.2]))

layer2 = NeuralLayer(weights=jnp.array([[0.5, 0.6], [0.7,
0.8]]),

                     biases=jnp.array([0.3, 0.4]))

# Create the neural network

model = NeuralNetwork(layers=[layer1, layer2])

# Register NeuralNetwork as a PyTree node
```

```
def nn_flatten(nn):
    leaves = nn.layers
    aux_data = {}
    return leaves, aux_data
def nn_unflatten(aux_data, leaves):
    return NeuralNetwork(layers=leaves)
tree_util.register_pytree_node(NeuralNetwork, nn_flatten,
nn_unflatten)
```

Now you can continue to train the model using JAX transformations:

```
# Define the loss function for the model
def model_loss_fn(model, x, y_true):
    y_pred = model(x)
    loss = jnp.mean((y_pred - y_true) ** 2)
    return loss
# Compute gradients with respect to the model parameters
model_grads = jax.grad(model_loss_fn)(model, x_data,
y_data)
# Update the model parameters
updated_model = jax.tree_map(update_params, model,
model_grads)
```

Use 'vmap' and other Transformations

Because your custom classes are now PyTree-compatible, you can use **vmap** to vectorize operations:

```
# Vectorize the forward pass over a batch of inputs

batched_forward = jax.vmap(forward_pass, in_axes=(None,
0))

# Apply to a batch of inputs

outputs = batched_forward(layer, x_data)

print("Batched Outputs:\n", outputs)
```

If your class contains static fields (data that should not be transformed), you can include them in the auxiliary data during flattening.

```
class NeuralLayerStatic:

    def __init__(self, weights, biases, activation_fn):

        self.weights = weights

        self.biases = biases

        self.activation_fn = activation_fn  # Static
field

    def __call__(self, x):

        z = jnp.dot(x, self.weights) + self.biases

        return self.activation_fn(z)

def layer_static_flatten(layer):

    leaves = (layer.weights, layer.biases)

    aux_data = layer.activation_fn

    return leaves, aux_data
```

```
def layer_static_unflatten(aux_data, leaves):
    return NeuralLayerStatic(*leaves,
activation_fn=aux_data)
tree_util.register_pytree_node(NeuralLayerStatic,
                               layer_static_flatten,
                               layer_static_unflatten)
```

By registering your custom classes as Pytrees, you enable JAX to recognize and manipulate them using its powerful functional transformations. This integration allows you to maintain clean, object-oriented code without sacrificing compatibility with JAX's ecosystem. You can now seamlessly include your custom classes in computations, apply transformations like **`jit`**, **`grad`**, and **`vmap`**, and utilize utilities like **`jax.tree_map`** for parameter updates.

Serializing and Deserializing Pytrees

For tasks like checkpointing during training, model persistence, or transferring models between environments, it's essential to save (serialize) and load (deserialize) Pytrees efficiently. However, since Pytrees can contain complex nested structures and custom objects, standard serialization methods may not suffice or could lead to inefficiencies. The challenge is to find effective methods to serialize and deserialize Pytrees, ensuring that model parameters are accurately saved and restored, thereby facilitating checkpointing and long-term storage.

To serialize and deserialize Pytrees, we can use libraries that handle complex data structures and support efficient storage formats. The most common approaches involve using:

- **Pickle**: A Python built-in module that serializes and deserializes Python objects. However, it's not always the most efficient or secure method.
- **MessagePack**: A binary serialization format that's faster and more efficient than JSON.
- **JAX's built-in utilities**: Functions like **`jax.tree_map`** and **`jax.tree_flatten`** can be combined with serialization libraries to handle Pytrees.
- **Custom serialization methods**: For user-defined classes registered as Pytrees, we may need to define custom serialization logic.

Here in this recipe, we'll focus on using **`flax.serialization`** which provides utilities for serializing and deserializing Pytrees efficiently. We'll learn to save and load model parameters organized as Pytrees.

To begin with, we first install Flax:

```
pip install flax
```

Understanding Model Parameters as Pytrees

Assume you have a model with parameters organized in a PyTree structure:

```
import jax

import jax.numpy as jnp

# Example model parameters as a PyTree

params = {

    'layer1': {

        'weights': jnp.array([[0.1, 0.2], [0.3, 0.4]]),

        'biases': jnp.array([0.1, 0.2])

    },

    'layer2': {

        'weights': jnp.array([[0.5, 0.6], [0.7, 0.8]]),

        'biases': jnp.array([0.3, 0.4])

    }

}
```

Import the necessary module:

```
from flax import serialization
```

Serializing PyTree to Bytes

Then, use **flax.serialization.to_bytes** to convert the PyTree into a bytes object suitable for saving to a file.

```
# Serialize the parameters to bytes

param_bytes = serialization.to_bytes(params)
```

Next, write the serialized bytes to a file using standard file I/O operations.

```
# Save to a file

with open('model_params.msgpack', 'wb') as f:

    f.write(param_bytes)
```

This saves the model parameters in a binary format using MessagePack, which is efficient and preserves the structure.

Loading and Deserializing PyTree

Now, to load the parameters back into a PyTree, read the bytes from the file and use **flax.serialization.from_bytes**.

```
# Read from the file

with open('model_params.msgpack', 'rb') as f:

    loaded_bytes = f.read()

# Deserialize the bytes back to a PyTree

# Provide an empty PyTree with the same structure as the
original

empty_params = jax.tree_map(lambda x: jnp.zeros_like(x),
params)

# Deserialize
```

```
loaded_params = serialization.from_bytes(empty_params, loaded_bytes)
```

Here, since the deserialization process requires knowledge of the structure, we provide an empty PyTree (**empty_params**) with the same structure as the original.

Here, ensure that the loaded parameters match the original ones.

```
# Verify that the parameters are the same

def compare_params(p1, p2):

    return all([jnp.allclose(a, b) for a, b in zip(jax.tree_leaves(p1), jax.tree_leaves(p2))])

print("Parameters match:", compare_params(params, loaded_params))
```

Handling Custom Classes in Pytrees

If your PyTree contains user-defined classes registered as Pytrees, ensure they are serializable. For custom classes, you may need to implement custom serialization methods.

Check the following example on custom class:

```
class NeuralLayer:

    def __init__(self, weights, biases):

        self.weights = weights

        self.biases = biases

    # ... (methods omitted for brevity)
```

Then, register the class as a PyTree node:

```
from jax import tree_util

def neural_layer_flatten(layer):
```

```
    # The leaves are the parameters we want to serialize
    leaves = (layer.weights, layer.biases)
    # Auxiliary data can be any static data needed to
reconstruct the object
    aux_data = None
    return leaves, aux_data
def neural_layer_unflatten(aux_data, leaves):
    return NeuralLayer(*leaves)
tree_util.register_pytree_node(NeuralLayer,
neural_layer_flatten, neural_layer_unflatten)
```

For serialization, you may need to define how to serialize and deserialize your custom classes.

Serializing and Deserializing PyTree with Custom Classes

Now, you can serialize and deserialize the PyTree containing your custom classes. Given below is the sample program:

```
# Create a PyTree with custom classes
params_custom = {
    'layer1': NeuralLayer(weights=jnp.array([[0.1, 0.2],
[0.3, 0.4]]),
                            biases=jnp.array([0.1, 0.2])),
    'layer2': NeuralLayer(weights=jnp.array([[0.5, 0.6],
[0.7, 0.8]]),
                            biases=jnp.array([0.3, 0.4]))
}
```

```
# Serialize to bytes

param_bytes_custom =
serialization.to_bytes(params_custom)

# Save to a file

with open('model_params_custom.msgpack', 'wb') as f:

    f.write(param_bytes_custom)

# Load from the file

with open('model_params_custom.msgpack', 'rb') as f:

    loaded_bytes_custom = f.read()

# Provide an empty PyTree template

empty_params_custom = jax.tree_map(lambda x:
NeuralLayer(jnp.zeros_like(x.weights),
jnp.zeros_like(x.biases)), params_custom)

# Deserialize

loaded_params_custom =
serialization.from_bytes(empty_params_custom,
loaded_bytes_custom)
```

Saving and Loading Checkpoints during Training

In practice, you may want to save checkpoints periodically during training. Check the following example:

```
# Training loop

num_epochs = 10

for epoch in range(num_epochs):
```

```
    # ... training code ...
    # Save checkpoint every 5 epochs
    if (epoch + 1) % 5 == 0:
        param_bytes = serialization.to_bytes(params)
        with open(f'checkpoint_epoch_{epoch+1}.msgpack',
'wb') as f:
            f.write(param_bytes)
```

Next, perform to load from a checkpoint:

```
# Load parameters from a specific checkpoint
with open('checkpoint_epoch_5.msgpack', 'rb') as f:
    loaded_bytes = f.read()
params = serialization.from_bytes(empty_params,
loaded_bytes)
```

Using 'flax.training.checkpoints' Module

Flax also provides a higher-level API for managing checkpoints as below:

```
from flax.training import checkpoints
# Save a checkpoint
checkpoints.save_checkpoint(ckpt_dir='./checkpoints',
target=params, step=epoch)
# Restore from the latest checkpoint
```

```
restored_params =
checkpoints.restore_checkpoint(ckpt_dir='./checkpoints',
target=empty_params)
```

By utilizing **flax.serialization** and **flax.training.checkpoints**, you can effectively serialize and deserialize Pytrees containing model parameters, including those with custom classes. This capability allows you to save and load models accurately, facilitating checkpointing during training and long-term model persistence.

Filtering Pytrees for Specific Parameters

Sometimes, you may need to apply updates or transformations only to specific parameters within a Pytree, such as applying different learning rates to different layers, freezing certain layers during training, or modifying only weights and not biases. The challenge is to implement techniques that can traverse the Pytree and selectively modify or extract elements based on certain criteria, without affecting the rest of the structure.

To selectively modify elements within a Pytree, you can use JAX's tree traversal utilities, such as **jax.tree_map** and **jax.tree_leaves**, combined with filtering functions that identify the parameters of interest. By defining custom functions that can recognize and operate only on specific parts of the Pytree, you can apply updates selectively.

Let us consider a Pytree representing model parameters organized as nested dictionaries:

```
import jax

import jax.numpy as jnp

# Example model parameters

params = {

    'layer1': {

        'weights': jnp.array([[0.1, 0.2], [0.3, 0.4]]),

        'biases': jnp.array([0.1, 0.2]),

    },

    'layer2': {
```

```
        'weights': jnp.array([[0.5, 0.6], [0.7, 0.8]]),
        'biases': jnp.array([0.3, 0.4]),
    },
    'layer3': {
        'weights': jnp.array([[0.9, 1.0], [1.1, 1.2]]),
        'biases': jnp.array([0.5, 0.6]),
    },
}
```

In this example, **`params`** is a Pytree with three layers, each containing **`weights`** and **`biases`**.

Defining Filter Function

Now create a function that determines whether a parameter should be updated based on a condition. For instance, suppose you want to update only the **`weights`** and not the **`biases`**.

```
def is_weight(param_name):
    return 'weights' in param_name
```

Traversing Pytree with 'jax.tree_map' and Filtering

Since **`jax.tree_map`** doesn't provide access to the parameter names directly, we need to use custom traversal functions that include the paths.

```
def tree_map_with_path(f, tree):
    def helper(path, subtree):
        if isinstance(subtree, dict):
            return {k: helper(path + (k,), v) for k, v in
subtree.items()}
```

```
        else:
            return f(path, subtree)
    return helper((), tree)
```

Applying Updates selectively based on Parameter Names

Create an update function that uses the path to decide whether to update a parameter.

```
learning_rate = 0.01
def update_param(path, param):
    # path is a tuple of keys leading to the param
    if 'weights' in path:
        # Apply the update to weights
        grad = compute_gradient_for_param(param)  #
Placeholder for gradient computation
        return param - learning_rate * grad
    else:
        # Do not update biases; return the original param
        return param
```

Do not forget to replace **compute_gradient_for_param(param)** with the actual gradient for that parameter.

Next, use the custom traversal function to apply updates.

```
updated_params = tree_map_with_path(update_param, params)
```

Integrating with Gradient Computation

Assuming you have computed gradients in the same structure as **params**, you can modify the **update_param** function to include gradients.

```
def update_param_with_grad(path, param, grad):
    if 'weights' in path:
        return param - learning_rate * grad
    else:
        return param
```

Now, create a function to traverse both **params** and **grads** together.

```
def tree_map_with_path_and_grad(f, tree, grads):
    def helper(path, subtree, grad_subtree):
        if isinstance(subtree, dict):
            return {k: helper(path + (k,), v,
grad_subtree[k]) for k, v in subtree.items()}
        else:
            return f(path, subtree, grad_subtree)
    return helper((), tree, grads)
```

Then, apply the function:

```
updated_params =
tree_map_with_path_and_grad(update_param_with_grad,
params, grads)
```

Next, check that only the weights have been updated.

```
# Access updated weights and biases
```

```
print("Updated layer1 weights:",
updated_params['layer1']['weights'])

print("Original layer1 biases:",
updated_params['layer1']['biases'])  # Should be
unchanged
```

Generalizing Filter Function

Suppose you want to freeze the parameters of certain layers, e.g., freeze **layer1** and update only **layer2** and **layer3**.

For this, modify the **update_param_with_grad** function:

```
def update_param_with_grad(path, param, grad):

    if 'layer1' in path:

        # Do not update parameters in layer1

        return param

    else:

        # Update other layers

        return param - learning_rate * grad
```

Then, apply the update.

```
updated_params =
tree_map_with_path_and_grad(update_param_with_grad,
params, grads)
```

Using Regular Expressions for Complex Filters

For more complex filtering, you can use regular expressions to match parameter names.

```
import re
```

```
def update_param_with_regex(path, param, grad, pattern):
    param_name = '/'.join(path)
    if re.match(pattern, param_name):
        # Update parameters matching the pattern
        return param - learning_rate * grad
    else:
        # Do not update other parameters
        return param
pattern = r'^layer[23]/weights$'  # Example pattern
updated_params = tree_map_with_path_and_grad(
    lambda path, param, grad:
update_param_with_regex(path, param, grad, pattern),
    params,
    grads
)
```

Now, suppose you want to apply different learning rates to different layers.

```
def update_param_with_variable_lr(path, param, grad):
    if 'layer1' in path:
        lr = 0.01
    elif 'layer2' in path:
        lr = 0.001
```

```
    else:
        lr = 0.0001
    return param - lr * grad
updated_params =
tree_map_with_path_and_grad(update_param_with_variable_lr
, params, grads)
```

Using 'optax' for Parameter Masks

Alternatively, you can use the **optax** library to define parameter masks and apply optimizers selectively.

```
import optax
# Define parameter masks
def mask_fn(params):
    masks = {}
    def create_mask(path, param):
        if 'weights' in path:
            return True  # Update weights
        else:
            return False  # Do not update biases
    masks = tree_map_with_path(create_mask, params)
    return masks
# Create an optimizer with masks
optimizer = optax.chain(
```

```
    optax.masked(optax.sgd(learning_rate=0.01),
mask_fn(params))

)

# Initialize optimizer state

opt_state = optimizer.init(params)

# Compute updates

updates, opt_state = optimizer.update(grads, opt_state,
params)

# Apply updates

updated_params = optax.apply_updates(params, updates)
```

Combining Multiple Masks

You can now create complex masks by combining multiple conditions.

```
def mask_fn(params):

    def create_mask(path, param):

        if 'layer1' in path and 'weights' in path:

            return True  # Update weights in layer1

        elif 'layer2' in path:

            return False  # Freeze layer2

        else:

            return True  # Update other parameters

    return tree_map_with_path(create_mask, params)

# Use the mask in the optimizer
```

```
optimizer = optax.chain(
    optax.masked(optax.sgd(learning_rate=0.01),
mask_fn(params))
)
```

Next, integrate selective parameter updates into your training loop.

```
# Training loop
for epoch in range(num_epochs):
    # Compute gradients
    grads = compute_gradients(params, data)
    # Update parameters selectively
    updates, opt_state = optimizer.update(grads,
opt_state, params)
    params = optax.apply_updates(params, updates)
    # ... rest of training loop ...
```

These methods afford flexibility in training models, regardless of whether freezing certain layers, applying different learning rates or updating only weights and not biases is required. The utilisation of custom traversal functions, parameter masks, and optax enables the efficient management of complex parameter structures, thereby facilitating more controlled and effective training processes.

Summary

In a nutshell, the chapter set out to tackle the challenge of managing complex nested data structures in JAX transformations head on. Pytrees allows functions to be mapped over nested containers without any issues, making it much easier to manipulate such data and reducing the need for recursive functions. We then moved on to the issue of custom classes not being compatible with JAX's Pytrees. JAX was able to recognize and traverse instances of custom classes during transformations by defining how these classes could be flattened and reconstructed. Next, we addressed the necessity of serializing and deserializing Pytrees. The chapter showed the most efficient ways to serialize and deserialize Pytrees, particularly using the **`flax.serialization`** library.

Finally, the chapter addressed the challenge of applying updates to specific parameters within a Pytree. We implemented techniques to traverse and selectively modify elements in a Pytree based on certain conditions or criteria. Selective manipulation is essential for scenarios such as applying different learning rates to different layers, freezing certain layers during training, or updating only specific types of parameters like weights but not biases. By defining custom traversal functions and utilizing filtering mechanisms, you can maintain the overall structure of the Pytree while modifying only the desired elements.

In summary, the chapter provided a comprehensive understanding of how to master Pytrees for data structures in JAX. It provided readers with the practical skills they need to manipulate nested data efficiently, integrate custom classes with JAX's Pytrees, serialize and deserialize complex data structures, and selectively update parameters within Pytrees.

CHAPTER 5: EXPORTING AND SERIALIZATION

Overview

In this chapter, we will cover the essential aspects of exporting and serializing models developed using Google JAX, with a particular focus on the Fashion-MNIST dataset. We start by examining the best ways to save trained models, making sure they can be quickly loaded and used for inference in different settings. These techniques enable you to persist model parameters and handle the necessary data structures involved in model deployment.

Next, we'll look at how to save and resume long-running jobs. This is essential for maintaining the progress of training processes that may take a long time or be interrupted. We implement the best checkpointing strategies to resume training without losing any progress, making sure it's done reliably and efficiently. We also examine methods for converting JAX models to other frameworks, facilitating interoperability and leveraging the strengths of different machine learning ecosystems.

Finally, you will learn how to serialize custom objects in JAX, including serializing complex data structures and user-defined classes. Throughout this chapter, you will gain the practical skills you need to export and serialize JAX models, so you can confidently deploy your machine learning solutions and share them with others.

Saving Trained Models for Deployment

After training a neural network model, you may need to deploy the model to a production environment for inference. However, unlike some other frameworks, JAX does not have a built-in, standardized method for exporting models, including both the architecture and the trained parameters. This can make it unclear how to save and load models for deployment. The situation here is to find an effective way to serialize both the model parameters and the architecture so that the trained model can be easily loaded and used in a production setting, and such that the model's performance during inference matches that observed during training.

So here, to deploy a trained JAX model, primarily, you need to save two main components:

- **Model Parameters (Weights and Biases)**: These are typically organized as Pytrees and can be serialized using flax.serialization.
- **Model Architecture**: Since JAX uses functional programming paradigms, the model architecture is defined by the functions you've written. To "save" the architecture, you can either save the source code or use serialization methods if you've used Flax or Haiku that support model serialization.

Here, in this recipe, we'll explore methods to save and load both the model parameters and the architecture so as to deploy your JAX model for production use.

Define and Train Model

Let us first define the model:

```
class FashionMNISTModel(nn.Module):
    @nn.compact
    def __call__(self, x):
        x = x.reshape((x.shape[0], -1))  # Flatten the
images
        x = nn.Dense(features=128)(x)
        x = nn.relu(x)
        x = nn.Dense(features=10)(x)
        x = nn.log_softmax(x)  # For classification
        return x
```

Then, load and prepare the data:

```
# Load the dataset
ds_builder = tfds.builder('fashion_mnist')
ds_builder.download_and_prepare()
train_ds =
tfds.as_numpy(ds_builder.as_dataset(split='train',
batch_size=-1))
test_ds =
tfds.as_numpy(ds_builder.as_dataset(split='test',
batch_size=-1))
# Convert to JAX arrays
train_images = jnp.array(train_ds['image']) / 255.0
```

```
train_labels = jnp.array(train_ds['label'])

test_images = jnp.array(test_ds['image']) / 255.0

test_labels = jnp.array(test_ds['label'])
```

Next, create a training function:

```
def create_train_state(rng, learning_rate):

    model = FashionMNISTModel()

    params = model.init(rng, jnp.ones([1, 28,
28]))['params']

    tx = optax.sgd(learning_rate)

    return
train_state.TrainState.create(apply_fn=model.apply,
params=params, tx=tx)
```

After this, define the loss and accuracy functions:

```
def compute_metrics(logits, labels):

    loss = jnp.mean(optax.softmax_cross_entropy(logits,
one_hot(labels, num_classes=10)))

    accuracy = jnp.mean(jnp.argmax(logits, -1) == labels)

    return {'loss': loss, 'accuracy': accuracy}

def one_hot(labels, num_classes):

    return jnp.eye(num_classes)[labels]
```

Then, start training the model:

```
@jit
```

```
def train_step(state, batch):
    def loss_fn(params):
        logits = state.apply_fn({'params': params},
batch['image'])
        loss =
jnp.mean(optax.softmax_cross_entropy(logits,
one_hot(batch['label'], 10)))
        return loss
    grads = grad(loss_fn)(state.params)
    state = state.apply_gradients(grads=grads)
    return state
# Prepare the training data
batch_size = 128
num_epochs = 5
steps_per_epoch = train_images.shape[0] // batch_size
rng = random.PRNGKey(0)
state = create_train_state(rng, learning_rate=0.1)
for epoch in range(num_epochs):
    perm = random.permutation(rng, train_images.shape[0])
    for i in range(steps_per_epoch):
        batch_idx = perm[i * batch_size:(i + 1) *
batch_size]
```

```
        batch = {'image': train_images[batch_idx],
'label': train_labels[batch_idx]}

        state = train_step(state, batch)

    print(f'Epoch {epoch + 1} completed.')
```

Save Model Parameters

After training, you need to save the model's parameters using **`flax.serialization.`**

```
from flax.training import checkpoints

# Save the checkpoint

ckpt_dir = './checkpoints'

checkpoints.save_checkpoint(ckpt_dir,
target=state.params, step=0, overwrite=True)
```

This saves the model parameters in a format that can be easily restored later.

Save and Load Model for Inference

In our case, since the model does not have any additional state beyond the parameters, saving the class definition is the best way. Then, we can load the model parameters and use the model for inference in our production environment.

To do this, we first load the parameters:

```
# Load the checkpoint

from flax.training import checkpoints

ckpt_dir = './checkpoints'

params = checkpoints.restore_checkpoint(ckpt_dir,
target=None)
```

Then, instantiate the model:

```
model = FashionMNISTModel()
```

Followed by, we define an inference function:

```
def predict(images):
    logits = model.apply({'params': params}, images)
    predictions = jnp.argmax(logits, axis=-1)
    return predictions
```

Next, we test the model on new data:

```
# Use test images for demonstration
sample_images = test_images[:10]
sample_labels = test_labels[:10]
predictions = predict(sample_images)
print("Predictions:", predictions)
print("Actual Labels:", sample_labels)
```

Deploy Model

Depending on the deployment target which can be a web server, cloud function or an embedded device, we need to:

- Set up a server or endpoint to receive input data and return predictions.
- Ensure that the environment is properly configured with all dependencies.
- Implement security and scalability measures as needed.

The given below is a quick example of model deployment:

```
# inference.py
from flask import Flask, request, jsonify
```

```
import jax
import jax.numpy as jnp
from flax import linen as nn
from flax.training import checkpoints
from model import FashionMNISTModel
app = Flask(__name__)
# Load the model parameters
ckpt_dir = './checkpoints'
params = checkpoints.restore_checkpoint(ckpt_dir,
target=None)
# Instantiate the model
model = FashionMNISTModel()
# JIT-compiled prediction function
@jax.jit
def predict(images):
    logits = model.apply({'params': params}, images)
    predictions = jnp.argmax(logits, axis=-1)
    return predictions
@app.route('/predict', methods=['POST'])
def predict_route():
    data = request.get_json()
```

```
    images = jnp.array(data['images']) / 255.0  #
Normalize if necessary

    preds = predict(images).tolist()

    return jsonify({'predictions': preds})

if __name__ == '__main__':

    app.run(host='0.0.0.0', port=8080)
```

Testing Deployment

Finally, to test, just send a request to the endpoint:

```
import requests

import json

# Sample data

sample_images = test_images[:2]

sample_images_list = sample_images.tolist()

# Send a POST request

response = requests.post('http://localhost:8080/predict',
json={'images': sample_images_list})

# Get the predictions

predictions = response.json()['predictions']

print("Predictions:", predictions)
```

If you follow these steps, you'll be able to save your trained JAX models and deploy them easily. Using Flax, we saw how it makes easier to persist models and share them, and to integrate them into applications.

Checkpointing Long-Running Jobs

If you don't save the model state regularly, unexpected things like power outages, system crashes, or preemptible cloud instances can cause you to lose your training progress. This can be a real waste of time and computing power. The goal is to set up a solid checkpointing plan that saves the model's state at regular intervals during training.

To avoid losing your training progress, you can set up checkpointing to save the model's parameters, optimizer state, and any other info needed to resume training at regular intervals. In JAX, you can use built-in utilities that serialize and deserialize the training state efficiently to make checkpointing easier.

Creating Training State

To begin with, first set up the training state for our defined neural network model, including the model parameters and optimizer.

```
def create_train_state(rng, learning_rate):

    model = FashionMNISTModel()

    params = model.init(rng, jnp.ones([1, 28,
28]))['params']

    tx = optax.adam(learning_rate)

    return
train_state.TrainState.create(apply_fn=model.apply,
params=params, tx=tx)
```

Next, define the loss and accuracy metrics:

```
def compute_metrics(logits, labels):

    loss =
optax.softmax_cross_entropy_with_integer_labels(logits,
labels).mean()

    accuracy = jnp.mean(jnp.argmax(logits, -1) == labels)
```

```
    return {'loss': loss, 'accuracy': accuracy}
```

Implementing Training Step

Next, we use **`jax.jit`** to compile the training step for efficiency.

```
@jit

def train_step(state, batch):

    def loss_fn(params):

        logits = FashionMNISTModel().apply({'params':
params}, batch['images'])

        loss =
optax.softmax_cross_entropy_with_integer_labels(logits,
batch['labels']).mean()

        return loss

    grads = grad(loss_fn)(state.params)

    state = state.apply_gradients(grads=grads)

    return state
```

Implementing Checkpointing

Then decide on a directory to store checkpoints and the frequency of saving.

```
ckpt_dir = './checkpoints'

checkpoint_frequency = 5  # Save a checkpoint every 5
epochs
```

Just tweak the training loop so it saves checkpoints every so often.

```
import os
```

```
num_epochs = 50  # Example for a long-running job

rng = random.PRNGKey(0)

state = create_train_state(rng, learning_rate=0.001)

# Restore from the latest checkpoint if available

state = checkpoints.restore_checkpoint(ckpt_dir,
target=state)

# Determine the starting epoch

start_epoch = int(state.step / len(train_ds))

for epoch in range(start_epoch, num_epochs):

    for batch in train_ds:

        state = train_step(state, batch)

    # Update the training step (epoch)

    state = state.replace(step=state.step +
len(train_ds))

    # Save a checkpoint every 'checkpoint_frequency'
epochs

    if (epoch + 1) % checkpoint_frequency == 0:

        checkpoints.save_checkpoint(ckpt_dir,
target=state, step=state.step, overwrite=True)

        print(f'Checkpoint saved at step {state.step}')

    # Optionally, evaluate on the test set

    # ... (evaluation code)
```

```
    print(f'Epoch {epoch + 1} completed.')
```

To quickly summarize the above script, the **checkpoints.save_checkpoint** function saves the entire training state, including model parameters and optimizer state. And, we set the **overwrite=True** to ensure that only the latest checkpoint is kept, so as to save disk space.

Handling Unexpected Interruptions

In the event of an interruption, you can resume training from the last saved checkpoint.

```
# Before starting the training loop

state = checkpoints.restore_checkpoint(ckpt_dir,
target=state)

# The rest of the training loop remains the same
```

Customizing Checkpointing Strategies

You can customize the checkpointing strategy based on your needs. You can keep the last N checkpoints and save the model when it achieves the best validation accuracy.

```
# In the evaluation section

if test_metrics['accuracy'] > best_accuracy:

    best_accuracy = test_metrics['accuracy']

    checkpoints.save_checkpoint(ckpt_dir, target=state,
step=state.step, prefix='best_', overwrite=True)

    print('Best model checkpoint saved.')
```

Once done, save the checkpoints asynchronously in order to avoid slowing down the whole training.

Testing Checkpoint Restoration

Now, before relying on checkpointing for long-running jobs, test that you can save and restore the training state correctly.

```
# Simulate interruption

checkpoints.save_checkpoint(ckpt_dir, target=state,
step=state.step, overwrite=True)

print('Simulating interruption...')

# Reset state

state = create_train_state(rng, learning_rate=0.001)

# Restore state

state = checkpoints.restore_checkpoint(ckpt_dir,
target=state)

print('State restored. Resuming training...')
```

If you use Flax's utilities to set up checkpoints, you can make sure you don't lose any progress if your training is interrupted. If you save the model's state regularly, you can pick up where you left off with the last checkpoint, which helps you avoid wasting computational effort. This is a must for long-running training jobs, especially when you're using preemptible cloud instances or working in environments where interruptions are common.

Converting JAX Models to Other Frameworks

Sometimes you might need to combine your JAX model with other machine learning frameworks or deploy it in places that don't support JAX straight away. For example, you might want to use a framework that offers specific tools or optimizations, or deploy your model to a platform that requires a standard format like ONNX (Open Neural Network Exchange). Since JAX doesn't directly support exporting models to formats that other frameworks can use, the challenge is to find a way to convert your JAX models into a format that can be used elsewhere, like ONNX, without losing the model's integrity or performance.

If you want to export a JAX model to a format that other frameworks like ONNX can use, you can use the jax2tf module. This converts JAX functions into TensorFlow operations. Once you've converted the model to TensorFlow, you can use TensorFlow's ONNX exporter to convert it to the ONNX format. This two-step process lets you connect JAX models with other ecosystems, giving you more deployment options.

To do this, let's consider a simple JAX model without using Flax.

```
import jax.numpy as jnp

def relu(x):

    return jnp.maximum(0, x)

def predict(params, x):

    W1, b1, W2, b2 = params

    x = x.reshape((x.shape[0], -1))  # Flatten the images

    z1 = jnp.dot(x, W1) + b1

    a1 = relu(z1)

    z2 = jnp.dot(a1, W2) + b2

    logits = z2

    return logits
```

Next, initialize the model parameters as below:

```
import numpy as np

input_size = 784  # 28x28 images flattened

hidden_size = 128

output_size = 10  # Number of classes

key = jax.random.PRNGKey(0)

W1 = jax.random.normal(key, (input_size, hidden_size))

b1 = jnp.zeros(hidden_size)
```

```
W2 = jax.random.normal(key, (hidden_size, output_size))

b2 = jnp.zeros(output_size)

params = [W1, b1, W2, b2]
```

Convert JAX Model to TensorFlow

To convert, first you need sample input data to trace the model during conversion.

```
# Sample input batch

x_sample = jnp.ones((1, 28, 28))  # A batch of one image
```

Next, import **jax2tf** and convert the **predict** function.

```
from jax.experimental import jax2tf

import tensorflow as tf

# Wrap the predict function to accept and return
TensorFlow tensors

def predict_tf(params, x):

    return jax2tf.convert(lambda x: predict(params,
x))(x)

# Convert the parameters to TensorFlow tensors

params_tf = [tf.convert_to_tensor(p) for p in params]

# Convert the sample input to TensorFlow tensor

x_sample_tf = tf.convert_to_tensor(np.array(x_sample),
dtype=tf.float32)
```

Build TensorFlow Function for Exporting

You can use TensorFlow's Function decorator to build a callable that can be exported.

```
@tf.function(input_signature=[tf.TensorSpec(shape=[None,
28, 28], dtype=tf.float32)])

def model_tf(x):

    return predict_tf(params_tf, x)
```

Convert TensorFlow Model to ONNX

Next, install the **tf2onnx** package if you haven't already.

```
pip install tf2onnx
```

Next, you'll want to export the model to ONNX.

```
import tf2onnx

# Convert the TensorFlow model to ONNX

spec = (tf.TensorSpec((None, 28, 28), tf.float32),)

output_path = "model.onnx"

# Perform the conversion

model_proto, _ = tf2onnx.convert.from_function(

    model_tf,

    input_signature=spec,

    opset=13,  # Specify the ONNX opset version

    output_path=output_path

)
```

You can use the **onnx** library to load and check the model.

```
import onnx

# Load the ONNX model

onnx_model = onnx.load(output_path)

# Check the model for errors

onnx.checker.check_model(onnx_model)

print("ONNX model is valid.")
```

Run Inference with ONNX Model

Make use of the **`onnxruntime`** to perform inference with the exported model.

```
pip install onnxruntime
```

Following is a quick inference example:

```
import onnxruntime as ort

import numpy as np

# Create an ONNX inference session

ort_session = ort.InferenceSession(output_path)

# Prepare input data

x_input = np.ones((1, 28, 28), dtype=np.float32)

# Run inference

outputs = ort_session.run(None, {'x': x_input})

# Get the output logits

logits = outputs[0]
```

```
print("Logits:", logits)
```

Compare JAX and ONNX Model Results

Ensure that the outputs from the JAX model and the ONNX model are consistent.

```
# Get JAX model output

jax_output = predict(params, x_sample)

# Compare with ONNX model output

print("JAX logits:", jax_output)

print("ONNX logits:", logits)

# Check if the outputs are close

are_close = np.allclose(np.array(jax_output), logits,
atol=1e-5)

print("Outputs are close:", are_close)
```

In this approach, the model parameters are hardcoded in the TensorFlow function. If you want a more flexible solution, especially for larger models, you might want to think about exporting the parameters separately.

After this, you can now deploy the ONNX model using any framework or platform that supports ONNX models.

Serializing Custom Objects in JAX

There are instances where you might create custom layers or objects that are not serializable by default. This can be problematic when you need to save your model's state, including these custom components, for purposes such as checkpointing, model persistence, or deployment. Standard serialization methods may fail or not adequately capture the necessary information to reconstruct these custom objects. The challenge is to develop a way to serialize and deserialize custom objects so that they can be saved and loaded seamlessly, preserving the model's functionality.

Now, to serialize custom objects, you can create custom serialization functions that define how your objects are converted to and from a serializable format. By implementing methods that specify how to extract the necessary data from your custom objects and how to reconstruct them, you can ensure that they can be saved and loaded correctly. Libraries like **`flax.serialization`** can be extended to handle custom serialization logic, allowing you to integrate with JAX's serialization ecosystem.

Define Custom Objects

Suppose you have a custom layer defined as a class:

```
import jax.numpy as jnp

from flax import linen as nn

class CustomLayer(nn.Module):

    features: int

    @nn.compact

    def __call__(self, x):

        W = self.param('W',
nn.initializers.lecun_normal(), (x.shape[-1],
self.features))

        b = self.param('b', nn.initializers.zeros,
(self.features,))

        return jnp.tanh(jnp.dot(x, W) + b)
```

Next, incorporate the custom layer into a model:

```
class CustomModel(nn.Module):

    @nn.compact

    def __call__(self, x):

        x = x.reshape((x.shape[0], -1))

        x = CustomLayer(features=128)(x)
```

```
        x = nn.Dense(features=10)(x)

        x = nn.log_softmax(x)

        return x
```

Initialize and Train Model

Then, set up the training loop as usual.

```
from flax.training import train_state

import optax

def create_train_state(rng, learning_rate):

    model = CustomModel()

    params = model.init(rng, jnp.ones([1, 28,
28]))['params']

    tx = optax.adam(learning_rate)

    return
train_state.TrainState.create(apply_fn=model.apply,
params=params, tx=tx)

# Initialize the training state

rng = jax.random.PRNGKey(0)

state = create_train_state(rng, learning_rate=0.001)

# ... Training loop ...
```

Serialize the Model

When you try to save the model parameters using **flax.serialization**, you might encounter issues due to the custom layer.

```
from flax.training import checkpoints

# Attempt to save the checkpoint

ckpt_dir = './checkpoints'

try:

    checkpoints.save_checkpoint(ckpt_dir,
target=state.params, step=0, overwrite=True)

except Exception as e:

    print("Serialization failed:", e)
```

Implement Custom Serialization Functions

To handle serialization of **CustomLayer**, you need to define how to convert it to a serializable state and how to restore it.

```
from flax.serialization import to_state_dict,
from_state_dict

def custom_layer_state_dict(layer):

    # Extract parameters

    return {'W': layer.W, 'b': layer.b}

def custom_layer_from_state_dict(layer, state):

    # Restore parameters

    layer.W = state['W']

    layer.b = state['b']

    return layer
```

Then, register the serialization functions:

```
from flax.serialization import
register_serialization_state

register_serialization_state(

    CustomLayer, custom_layer_state_dict,
custom_layer_from_state_dict

)
```

Now, save the model parameters using **`flax.serialization`**.

```
# Save the checkpoint

checkpoints.save_checkpoint(ckpt_dir,
target=state.params, step=0, overwrite=True)

print("Model parameters saved successfully.")
```

Load Model Parameters

When loading the model, ensure that the custom serialization logic is available.

```
# Restore the parameters

restored_params =
checkpoints.restore_checkpoint(ckpt_dir, target=None)
```

And then, instantiate the model and test it with the restored parameters.

```
model = CustomModel()

# Define an inference function

def predict(params, x):

    logits = model.apply({'params': params}, x)

    return logits
```

```
# Prepare sample input
x_sample = jnp.ones((1, 28, 28))
# Get predictions
logits = predict(restored_params, x_sample)
print("Logits:", logits)
```

Handle additional Custom Objects

If your custom objects contain non-serializable attributes (e.g., file handles, threads), exclude them from the state dict.

For example:

```
class CustomLayer(nn.Module):
    features: int
    non_serializable_attr: any =
nn.field(pytree_node=False)
    @nn.compact
    def __call__(self, x):
        # ... as before ...
        pass
```

This tells Flax not to include the attribute in the PyTree traversal, avoiding serialization issues.

Serialize Training State

You may also need to serialize the optimizer state and other training information.

```
# Save the entire training state
```

```
checkpoints.save_checkpoint(ckpt_dir, target=state,
step=state.step, overwrite=True)

# Restore the training state

restored_state = checkpoints.restore_checkpoint(ckpt_dir,
target=state)
```

For objects that cannot be easily represented as state dicts, consider implementing **`__getstate__`** and **`__setstate__`** methods.

For example:

```
class CustomObject:

    def __init__(self, data):

        self.data = data

        self.non_serializable = open('file.txt', 'r')

    def __getstate__(self):

        state = self.__dict__.copy()

        # Remove non-serializable entries

        del state['non_serializable']

        return state

    def __setstate__(self, state):

        self.__dict__.update(state)

        # Re-initialize non-serializable attributes

        self.non_serializable = open('file.txt', 'r')
```

If necessary, you can use **`pickle`** to serialize custom objects, but be cautious about security implications.

```
import pickle

# Serialize

with open('model.pkl', 'wb') as f:

    pickle.dump(state, f)

# Deserialize

with open('model.pkl', 'rb') as f:

    restored_state = pickle.load(f)
```

If you create your own serialization functions, you can handle objects that aren't standard. You can also set up ways to convert your custom objects to and from serializable formats. This makes it easier to save and load your models without any problems. This approach makes your model persistence strategy more reliable.

Summary

We thoroughly explored a variety of methods for exporting and serializing models developed with Google JAX. The chapter addressed the challenge of saving trained models for deployment head-on. We mastered the art of saving both the model architecture and parameters using Flax. We successfully persisted the model's state and ensured it could be loaded for inference in production environments.

We then moved on to checkpointing long-running jobs to prevent any loss of training progress due to unexpected interruptions. This strategy guarantees that training can resume from the last checkpoint without significant loss, enhancing the reliability of long-duration training sessions. The chapter also demonstrated how to convert JAX models to other frameworks, particularly using the jax2tf module to convert JAX functions into TensorFlow operations. By leveraging TensorFlow's ONNX exporter, we were able to deploy JAX models in environments where JAX isn't supported, broadening the applicability of our work.

Finally, we addressed the serialization of custom objects in JAX. We discovered that custom layers or classes are not serializable by default, which significantly hinders model persistence and deployment. We overcame this by creating custom serialization functions that define how to extract and restore the state of these objects. The chapter provided us with the essential techniques we needed to export, checkpoint, and interoperate with our models, as well as serialize custom objects. These techniques have greatly enhanced the portability and robustness of our JAX models.

Chapter 6: Type Promotion Semantics and Mixed Precision

Overview

In this chapter, we will explore the specifics of data types and precision in Google JAX, and how they affect memory usage and computational efficiency. We begin by examining the processes behind type promotion in arithmetic operations. This can result in unintentional increases in data type precision and, subsequently, memory consumption.

Next, we will look at mixed precision training, which is a technique that leverages both high and low-precision data types to accelerate training while maintaining model accuracy. We also address common type errors that arise in complex functions and provide effective strategies to debug and resolve these issues. The chapter introduces the essential use of custom data types, allowing for unparalleled control over numerical precision and performance optimization. By customizing data types, you can precisely tailor the computational characteristics of your model to align with specific hardware or application requirements.

Finally, we discuss effective methods to optimize memory usage by employing lower precision types where appropriate, striking the ideal balance between efficiency and accuracy. Throughout the chapter, you will see practical examples and solutions that equip you with the skills needed to confidently manage data types and precision in JAX.

Controlling Type Promotion in Arithmetic Operations

When working with JAX for machine learning tasks, you might encounter unintended type promotions during arithmetic operations. For example, performing calculations with mixed data types like **`float16`** and **`float32`** can result in automatic promotion to a higher precision type (**`float32`** or even **`float64`**). This promotion can increase memory usage and computational overhead, negating the benefits of using lower precision types. The challenge is to explicitly manage data types in your computations to prevent unwanted type promotions, ensuring that memory usage remains optimized without sacrificing numerical accuracy.

Now, to control type promotion, you need to:

1. Know how JAX handles operations between different data types.
2. Use casting functions to ensure variables are in the desired data type before operations.
3. Employ JAX's precision control settings to manage default behaviors.
4. Check and enforce data types at each step to prevent unintended promotions.

Understanding JAX's Type Promotion Rules

JAX follows NumPy's type promotion rules, which determine the output type when performing operations on inputs of different types.

- When combining integers and floating-point numbers, the result is promoted to a floating-point type.
- When performing operations between **float16** and **float32**, the result is promoted to **float32**.
- Including a **float64** in any operation will promote the result to **float64**.

Following is a quick example of unintended type promotion:

```
import jax.numpy as jnp

a = jnp.array([1.0, 2.0], dtype=jnp.float16)

b = jnp.array([3.0, 4.0], dtype=jnp.float32)

c = a + b

print(c.dtype)  # Output: float32
```

Here, adding a **float16** array to a **float32** array results in a **float32** output.

Explicitly Cast Data Types before Operations

To prevent unintended promotions, ensure all operands are of the same desired data type as below:

```
a = jnp.array([1.0, 2.0], dtype=jnp.float16)

b = jnp.array([3.0, 4.0], dtype=jnp.float32)

# Cast 'b' to float16 before the operation

b_cast = b.astype(jnp.float16)

c = a + b_cast

print(c.dtype)  # Output: float16
```

Now here, by casting **b** to **float16**, the addition operation retains the lower precision.

Consistent Data Types in Model Parameters

Here in this, you must ensure that all model parameters and inputs are consistently typed.

```
# Model weights initialization

key = jax.random.PRNGKey(0)

W1 = jax.random.normal(key, (784, 256),
dtype=jnp.float16)

b1 = jnp.zeros((256,), dtype=jnp.float16)

W2 = jax.random.normal(key, (256, 128),
dtype=jnp.float16)

b2 = jnp.zeros((128,), dtype=jnp.float16)

params = [W1, b1, W2, b2]
```

Casting Input Data and Enforcing Data Types

When loading data, cast it to the desired type.

```
# Load and preprocess data

train_images = ...  # Load data as NumPy array

train_images = train_images.astype(jnp.float16) / 255.0
# Normalize and cast
```

Ensure functions do not introduce unintended promotions.

```
def forward_pass(params, x):

    W1, b1, W2, b2 = params

    x = x.astype(jnp.float16)  # Ensure input is float16

    z1 = jnp.dot(x, W1) + b1
```

```
    a1 = jax.nn.relu(z1)
    z2 = jnp.dot(a1, W2) + b2
    y_pred = jax.nn.softmax(z2)
    return y_pred.astype(jnp.float16)
```

Using Context Managers for Precision Control

JAX also provides context managers to control default data types as demonstrated below:

```
from jax import config
config.update("jax_enable_x64", False)  # Disable float64
globally
```

This above setting forces all computations to use **float32** or lower precision, preventing unintended promotions to **float64**.

Monitoring Data Types during Computation

Now here, you can insert checks or print statements to monitor data types.

Following is a quick example:

```
def forward_pass(params, x):
    W1, b1, W2, b2 = params
    x = x.astype(jnp.float16)
    print("Input dtype:", x.dtype)
    z1 = jnp.dot(x, W1) + b1
    print("z1 dtype:", z1.dtype)
    # Continue with the rest of the computation
```

While you do, you may use **jax.debug** to enforce data type constraints during execution.

```
from jax import debug

def forward_pass(params, x):

    W1, b1, W2, b2 = params

    x = x.astype(jnp.float16)

    debug.assert_equal(x.dtype, jnp.float16, "Input x is not float16")

    z1 = jnp.dot(x, W1) + b1

    debug.assert_equal(z1.dtype, jnp.float16, "z1 is not float16")

    # Continue with the rest of the computation
```

Using Mixed Precision Training

Just a heads-up that using lower precision types like float16 might lead to numerical instability or reduce model accuracy. Keep an eye on how the model is performing and make any necessary adjustments. Below is a quick example on this limitation:

```
# Potential underflow or overflow in computations

small_values = jnp.array([1e-8, 1e-9], dtype=jnp.float16)

result = jnp.log(small_values)

print(result)  # May result in -inf or NaN
```

In cases where **float16** causes instability, you might use mixed precision training, where certain parts of the model use higher precision.

```
def forward_pass(params, x):

    W1, b1, W2, b2 = params

    x = x.astype(jnp.float16)
```

```
    z1 = jnp.dot(x, W1.astype(jnp.float16)) +
b1.astype(jnp.float16)

    a1 = jax.nn.relu(z1).astype(jnp.float32)  # Promote
to float32

    z2 = jnp.dot(a1, W2.astype(jnp.float32)) +
b2.astype(jnp.float32)

    y_pred = jax.nn.softmax(z2)

    return y_pred.astype(jnp.float32)
```

On hardware that supports **bfloat16**, such as TPUs, consider using it as it provides a wider dynamic range than **float16**.

```
x = x.astype(jnp.bfloat16)
```

If you follow these steps, you can easily manage data types in your JAX computations to avoid any unexpected type promotions. This control helps cut down on memory usage and can make computations more efficient, especially when you're working with big models or datasets. It's important to consider the pros and cons of lower precision. On the one hand, it can save you memory, but on the other, it might affect how stable your numbers are and how accurate your model is.

Implementing Mixed Precision Training

Training deep neural networks can be pretty time-consuming, especially with large models. You might notice that training is slow, and you want to speed it up without losing too much accuracy in the model. One great way to speed things up is mixed precision training, which uses both 16-bit and 32-bit floating-point types to make computations faster and use less memory. The goal is to implement mixed precision training in JAX in a way that speeds up computations while keeping the numbers stable and the model performing well.

Mixed precision training leverages lower precision data types (like **float16** or **bfloat16**) for most computations to speed up processing and reduce memory consumption. Critical parts of the computation that require higher precision use **float32**. If you manage your data types carefully, you can get faster training times while keeping the model's accuracy as good as it would be with full precision training.

Implement Loss Function

Now to begin, first load the training state of the model and then implement the loss function.

```
def compute_loss(params, images, labels):

    logits = FashionMNISTModel().apply({'params':
params}, images)

    loss =
optax.softmax_cross_entropy_with_integer_labels(logits,
labels).mean()

    return loss
```

Now here, we need to ensure that:

- Gradients are computed in **`float32`** to prevent underflow.
- Parameters are updated in **`float32`**.

```
@jit

def train_step(state, batch):

    images = batch['images']

    labels = batch['labels']


    def loss_fn(params):

        loss = compute_loss(params, images, labels)

        return loss


    grad_fn = value_and_grad(loss_fn)
```

```
    loss, grads = grad_fn(state.params)

    # Cast gradients to float32
    grads = jax.tree_map(lambda g: g.astype(jnp.float32),
grads)

    # Update state
    state = state.apply_gradients(grads=grads)
    return state, loss
```

Next, following is the training loop:

```
rng = jax.random.PRNGKey(0)
state = create_train_state(rng, learning_rate=0.001)
num_epochs = 10
for epoch in range(num_epochs):
    for batch in train_ds:
        state, loss = train_step(state, batch)
    print(f'Epoch {epoch + 1}, Loss: {loss}')
```

Then, implement the evaluation step:

```
@jit
def eval_step(params, batch):
    images = batch['images']
```

```
    labels = batch['labels']

    logits = FashionMNISTModel().apply({'params':
params}, images)

    loss =
optax.softmax_cross_entropy_with_integer_labels(logits,
labels).mean()

    accuracy = jnp.mean(jnp.argmax(logits, -1) == labels)

    return {'loss': loss, 'accuracy': accuracy}
```

And then, evaluate the model:

```
def evaluate_model(state, test_ds):

    metrics = []

    for batch in test_ds:

        metrics.append(eval_step(state.params, batch))

    metrics_np = jax.device_get(metrics)

    test_loss = np.mean([m['loss'] for m in metrics_np])

    test_accuracy = np.mean([m['accuracy'] for m in
metrics_np])

    print(f"Test Loss: {test_loss}, Test Accuracy:
{test_accuracy}")
```

Monitoring Model Accuracy

After training, compare the model's accuracy with that of a model trained with full precision to ensure there's no significant loss. See the following code snippet:

```
# Evaluate mixed precision model
```

```
evaluate_model(state, test_ds)

# Compare with full precision model (if available)

# ... (train and evaluate a full precision model)
```

Using 'bfloat16' on TPUs

If training on TPUs, then we need to replace **float16** with **bfloat16** for better dynamic range.

```
# Modify the model to use bfloat16

class FashionMNISTModel(nn.Module):

    @nn.compact

    def __call__(self, x):

        x = x.astype(jnp.bfloat16)

        # ... rest of the model ...
```

By using mixed-precision training, you can cut training times in half and reduce memory usage without losing any accuracy. It's really important to handle data types carefully and make sure you're doing the right level of calculation to get the results you want with mixed precision training.

Debugging Type Errors in Complex Functions

When developing complex functions in JAX, especially those involving multiple transformations and data manipulations, you may encounter unexpected data type errors. These errors can manifest as exceptions during execution or as silent failures leading to incorrect results. Diagnosing and fixing these type-related errors can be challenging due to JAX's functional programming paradigm and JIT compilation. The challenge is to systematically identify the source of type errors and implement solutions to resolve them, ensuring that your functions operate correctly.

Now here to debug type errors in complex JAX functions:

1. Be familiar with typical type-related issues in JAX.
2. Ensure that variables have the expected data types.

3. Use **`jax.debug`** utilities to inspect data types during execution.
4. Isolate parts of the function to pinpoint where the error occurs.
5. Be aware of limitations and constraints when using **`jit`**.

Recognize Common Type Errors

Typical type errors in JAX include:

- **Mismatched Data Types**: Operations between incompatible types (e.g., int32 and float32).
- **Unintended Type Promotions**: Implicit promotion to higher precision types.
- **Immutable Types**: Attempting to modify immutable arrays.

Let us consider following as one of the error message:

```
TypeError: Can't multiply sequence by non-int of type
'float'
```

Just make sure you cast your variables to the right data type.

```
def compute_area(length, width):

    length = jnp.asarray(length, dtype=jnp.float32)

    width = jnp.asarray(width, dtype=jnp.float32)

    area = length * width

    return area
```

Insert Debugging Statements

Now here, use **`jax.debug.print`** to output data types and shapes during execution.

```
from jax import debug

def complex_function(x):

    x = x.astype(jnp.float32)

    debug.print("x dtype: {}", x.dtype)
```

```
    # Perform operations
    y = x * 2.0
    debug.print("y dtype: {}", y.dtype)
    return y
```

Just a heads-up, when you're using JIT, it's important to make sure debug.print is compatible with compiled functions.

Simplify Function

Split the complicated function into more simple parts to spot the issue as shown below:

```
def complex_function(x):
    # Part 1
    x1 = part1(x)
    # Part 2
    x2 = part2(x1)
    # Part 3
    result = part3(x2)
    return result
```

Then, test each part individually. And while you do, ensure that operations are valid for the data types involved.

```
def safe_division(a, b):
    a = a.astype(jnp.float32)
    b = b.astype(jnp.float32)
    result = a / b
```

```
    return result
```

Next, ensure that inputs to the function have the correct data types and shapes as demonstrated below.

```
def process_input(data):

    if not isinstance(data, jnp.ndarray):

        data = jnp.array(data)

    if data.dtype != jnp.float32:

        data = data.astype(jnp.float32)

    return data
```

And do not forget to include assertions to enforce data type expectations. Following is a quick sample of adding assertions.

```
def compute_sum(a, b):

    assert a.dtype == b.dtype, "Data types of 'a' and 'b' must match"

    return a + b
```

It's important to remember that JIT-compiled functions can't include certain Python constructs or side effects.

Handle Python Scalar Types

You also have to be cautious with Python integers and floats, which may not match JAX types. For example:

```
def scale_array(x, scale):

    scale = jnp.asarray(scale, dtype=x.dtype)
```

```
    return x * scale
```

Use 'jax.numpy' Functions

I would suggest using jax.numpy functions instead of the Python built-ins, just to make sure everything's compatible as shown below:

```
def compute_sqrt(x):
    return jnp.sqrt(x)
```

If you're having trouble with the type error, you might want to check out some community forums or documentation.

Using Custom Data Types

In certain machine learning applications, standard data types like **`float32`** or **`float64`** may not suffice due to specific precision requirements or the need for specialized numerical behavior. For example, you might require fixed-point arithmetic, custom rounding behaviors, or representations optimized for specific hardware. JAX, by default, supports standard numerical types, but to meet the specialized needs of your project, you need to implement and utilize custom data types within JAX's framework. Here, the challenge is to integrate these custom types into JAX so that they can participate in JAX's transformations while ensuring correct and efficient computation.

So to use custom data types, you can define a new data type by creating a subclass of **`jax.lax_dtype`** or by using the **`jax.custom_dtype`** mechanism. Just to flag: JAX isn't set up to work with custom data types. As an alternative, you can simulate custom data types by representing them with standard types and overloading the necessary operations. As another option, you can use JAX's support for custom JVPs (Jacobian-vector products) and VJPs (vector-Jacobian products) to define custom behavior during automatic differentiation for certain use cases.

In this recipe, we'll explore how to implement custom data types using **Custom VJP** and **Custom JVP** functions, in order to define custom forward and backward behaviors for functions involving your specialized numerical types.

Simulating Custom Data Types

To begin with, our approach will be to simulate custom data types using existing types. For example, you can represent a fixed-point number using an integer type and define operations accordingly.

Suppose you want to implement fixed-point arithmetic with a specific scaling factor.

```
import jax

import jax.numpy as jnp

# Define a fixed-point class

class FixedPoint:

    def __init__(self, value, scale=1000):

        self.value = jnp.asarray(value)

        self.scale = scale


    def to_float(self):

        return self.value / self.scale


    def __add__(self, other):

        return FixedPoint(self.value + other.value,
self.scale)


    def __mul__(self, other):

        return FixedPoint((self.value * other.value) //
self.scale, self.scale)


    # Add other necessary methods...
```

```
# Example usage
a = FixedPoint(1000)  # Represents 1.0
b = FixedPoint(2000)  # Represents 2.0
c = a + b  # Represents 3.0
d = a * b  # Represents 2.0
```

Using JAX Custom Transforms

Now, to integrate custom operations with JAX, you can use **jax.custom_jvp** or **jax.custom_vjp** decorators to define custom forward and backward passes.

Suppose you have a function that operates on your custom data type, and you want to define how it should behave during differentiation.

Consider the following example of a custom square function:

```
@jax.custom_jvp
def custom_square(x):
    return x ** 2
# Define the custom JVP rule
@custom_square.defjvp
def custom_square_jvp(primals, tangents):
    x, = primals
    x_dot, = tangents
    primal_out = custom_square(x)
    tangent_out = 2 * x * x_dot  # Derivative of x^2 is
2x
    return primal_out, tangent_out
```

```
x = jnp.array(3.0)
y = custom_square(x)
dy_dx = jax.grad(custom_square)(x)
print("y =", y)             # y = 9.0
print("dy/dx =", dy_dx)  # dy/dx = 6.0
```

We also need to ensure that our custom data types can be used with JAX transformations. For this, let's define a custom data type for fixed-point numbers that can be differentiated.

```
    # Define JVP rules
    @add.defjvp
    def add_jvp(primals, tangents):
        a, b = primals
        a_dot, b_dot = tangents
        primal_out = FixedPoint.add(a, b)
        tangent_out = a_dot + b_dot
        return primal_out, tangent_out

    @multiply.defjvp
    def multiply_jvp(primals, tangents):
        a, b = primals
        a_dot, b_dot = tangents
        primal_out = FixedPoint.multiply(a, b)
```

```
        tangent_out = (a_dot * b.value + b_dot * a.value)
// a.scale
        return primal_out, tangent_out
```

Using Custom Data Type

Now, you can use **FixedPoint** in computations and apply **jax.grad**.

```
def compute(a_value, b_value):
    a = FixedPoint(a_value)
    b = FixedPoint(b_value)
    c = FixedPoint.multiply(a, b)
    return c.value
# Compute gradient with respect to a_value
grad_fn = jax.grad(compute)
gradient = grad_fn(1000.0, 2000.0)  # Inputs are scaled
integers
print("Gradient:", gradient)
```

Using Custom Pytrees

You can also represent your custom data type as a PyTree so that JAX can traverse it.

```
from jax import tree_util
def fixedpoint_flatten(fp):
    return (fp.value,), fp.scale
def fixedpoint_unflatten(scale, value):
```

```
    return FixedPoint(value[0], scale)
tree_util.register_pytree_node(FixedPoint,
fixedpoint_flatten, fixedpoint_unflatten)
```

Now, you can use JAX functions on FixedPoint instances

```
def compute_sum(a_value, b_value):
    a = FixedPoint(a_value)
    b = FixedPoint(b_value)
    c = a.value + b.value
    return c
grad_fn = jax.grad(compute_sum)
gradient = grad_fn(1000.0, 2000.0)
print("Gradient:", gradient)
```

This approach allows JAX to handle **`FixedPoint`** instances in transformations, but you still need to ensure that operations are correctly defined and compatible with JAX's expectations.For advanced use cases, you can define custom primitives as shown below:

```
def compute(a_value, b_value, scale=1000):
    a = jnp.asarray(a_value)
    b = jnp.asarray(b_value)
    c = fixed_mul(a, b, scale)
    return c
grad_fn = jax.grad(compute)
gradient = grad_fn(1000.0, 2000.0)
```

```
print("Gradient:", gradient)
```

If you use JAX's custom transformations and primitives with custom data types, you can make JAX do more for you, especially when it comes to handling special numerical situations. This approach requires you to think carefully about how you define operations and differentiate between them. But it lets you integrate custom types into JAX's ecosystem, which means you can use its automatic differentiation and compilation features.

Optimizing Memory with Lower Precision Types

Now, when working with large models or datasets, high-precision data types like **`float64`** can consume significant amounts of memory, leading to resource constraints and reduced performance. This is especially problematic when training deep neural networks where memory bandwidth is a bottleneck. To address this, you want to strategically use lower precision data types (like **`float16`** or **`bfloat16`**) where acceptable, to reduce memory footprint and potentially improve computational speed.

Analyzing Model and Data

So first, examine your model to identify components that can operate in lower precision:

- Weights and Activations: Often can be in lower precision.
- Gradients: May need higher precision to prevent underflow.
- Loss Computation: Typically requires higher precision.

Loading Data in Lower Precision

We need to tweak the data loading process to use lower precision types. For example:

```
import jax.numpy as jnp

# Load data as float16

train_images = ...  # Load as NumPy array

train_images = train_images.astype(jnp.float16) / 255.0
# Normalize

train_labels = ...  # Labels can remain as integers
```

Defining Model with Lower Precision Parameters

Just tweak the model definitions to use lower-precision data types using Flax:

```
from flax import linen as nn

class LowPrecisionModel(nn.Module):

    @nn.compact

    def __call__(self, x):

        x = x.astype(jnp.float16)

        x = x.reshape((x.shape[0], -1))

        x = nn.Dense(features=256, dtype=jnp.float16)(x)

        x = nn.relu(x)

        x = nn.Dense(features=128, dtype=jnp.float16)(x)

        x = nn.relu(x)

        x = nn.Dense(features=10, dtype=jnp.float16)(x)

        x = x.astype(jnp.float32)  # Convert to float32
for loss computation

        return x
```

Adjusting Optimizer

Here, use Optax so as to handle lower precision parameters.

```
import optax

def create_optimizer(learning_rate):

    # Use an optimizer that supports lower precision
```

```
    optimizer = optax.adam(learning_rate=learning_rate,
b1=0.9, b2=0.999, eps=1e-8)

    return optimizer
```

Modifying Training Step

Next, make sure the gradients are calculated at a higher precision.

```
@jax.jit

def train_step(state, batch):

    images = batch['images']

    labels = batch['labels']


    def loss_fn(params):

        loss = scaled_loss(params, images, labels)

        return loss

    grads = jax.grad(loss_fn)(state.params)

    grads = jax.tree_map(lambda g: g.astype(jnp.float32),
grads)  # Cast gradients to float32

    state = state.apply_gradients(grads=grads)

    return state
```

Just to make sure we're on the same page here, we need to initialise the model parameters to the desired precision.

```
def create_train_state(rng, learning_rate):

    model = LowPrecisionModel()
```

```
    params = model.init(rng, jnp.ones([1, 28, 28],
dtype=jnp.float16))['params']

    optimizer = create_optimizer(learning_rate)

    state =
train_state.TrainState.create(apply_fn=model.apply,
params=params, tx=optimizer)

    return state
```

Training Model

Then, proceed with the training loop as usual, and followed by evaluation of model performance.

```
rng = jax.random.PRNGKey(0)

state = create_train_state(rng, learning_rate=0.001)

for epoch in range(num_epochs):

    for batch in train_ds:

        state = train_step(state, batch)

    print(f"Epoch {epoch + 1} completed.")

#model performance evaluation

def evaluate_model(state, test_ds):

    total_loss = 0.0

    total_accuracy = 0.0

    for batch in test_ds:

        images = batch['images'].astype(jnp.float16)

        labels = batch['labels']
```

```
        logits = LowPrecisionModel().apply({'params':
state.params}, images)

        loss =
optax.softmax_cross_entropy_with_integer_labels(logits,
labels).mean()

        accuracy = jnp.mean(jnp.argmax(logits, -1) ==
labels)

        total_loss += loss

        total_accuracy += accuracy

    print(f"Test Loss: {total_loss}, Test Accuracy:
{total_accuracy}")

evaluate_model(state, test_ds)
```

Utilizing 'bfloat16' on TPUs

If you want to get the most out of TPUs, use bfloat16. You'll get better numerical properties with lower precision that way.

```
class LowPrecisionModel(nn.Module):

    @nn.compact

    def __call__(self, x):

        x = x.astype(jnp.bfloat16)

        # ... rest of the model ...
```

If you use lower precision data types in a smart way, you can cut down on memory use a lot and maybe even speed up the processing. It's important to think through these changes carefully to make sure the model stays accurate and stable. It's important to test and validate regularly to make sure that the benefits of reduced memory usage don't come at the cost of degraded performance.

Summary

We successfully explored data type management and precision in JAX, optimizing memory usage and computational efficiency. We started by tackling the issue of unintended type promotions in arithmetic operations. We knew that such promotions could lead to increased memory consumption and slower computations, and we were determined to find a solution. By explicitly managing data types and using consistent casting, we learned to prevent automatic promotions and maintain control over our numerical precision.

We found that implementing mixed-precision training is a highly effective technique for accelerating computations. We achieved faster training times without significant loss of accuracy by using lower precision types like float16 for most operations and reserving float32 for critical calculations. We also successfully addressed the challenge of debugging type errors in complex functions. By systematically diagnosing, explicitly casting types, and leveraging JAX's debugging tools, we were able to identify and resolve data type issues that could cause functions to fail unexpectedly. This proved the necessity of meticulous attention to data types throughout code development.

The chapter then moved on to the implementation of custom data types within JAX's framework, acknowledging scenarios where specialized numeric types are necessary. We integrated custom data types into JAX's automatic differentiation system by leveraging custom VJP and JVP functions. Finally, we optimized memory usage by employing lower precision types where appropriate. We effectively reduced the memory footprint of our models by adjusting data loading, model definitions, and computational precision.

CHAPTER 7: INTEGRATING FOREIGN FUNCTIONS (FFI)

Overview

In this chapter, we are going to dive right in and look at how to integrate foreign functions (FFI) within JAX to give you the best of the both worlds: enhanced functionality and performance, all in one neat package, in your machine learning models. We start by showing you how to call external C libraries directly from JAX. This lets you use optimized existing code for specific computations that aren't in JAX's standard library.

Next, we'll show you how to optimize performance using custom CUDA kernels. Standard operations simply don't cut it when it comes to GPU computations. That's why writing custom CUDA kernels is essential. We will show you how to create and integrate these kernels via FFI to get the best performance on your GPU hardware. We also tackle the issue of data conversion between JAX and external code head-on. Furthermore, we will show you how to manage thread safety and concurrency, which is crucial when working with external libraries that may not be thread-safe by default.

Finally, we will show you how to distribute computations across heterogeneous systems. You can optimize computations across different hardware resources effectively by leveraging JAX's capabilities alongside external functions.

Calling External C Libraries

While you're building machine learning models with JAX, you might find yourself needing to use existing C libraries for specific calculations that aren't available or efficient in JAX. These libraries might have some pretty specialized algorithms, legacy code, or highly optimized functions that can really boost your model's performance. The tricky part is making sure that JAX and C code work well together. We need to make sure that JAX's JIT compilation and automatic differentiation work with C code, but we also need to make sure that it's efficient.

JAX has ways to call external C functions using its Foreign Function Interface (FFI). You can use ctypes or cffi in Python to wrap C functions and make them accessible within JAX computations. You can also create your own JAX primitives to connect with these C functions. This lets you add them to JAX's computation graph, and it also allows JIT compilation and differentiation.

Prepare C Library

Let's assume you have a C function that computes the element-wise exponential of an array.

```
// custom_math.c

#include <math.h>

void custom_exp(int n, const double* x, double* y) {
```

```
    for (int i = 0; i < n; ++i) {
        y[i] = exp(x[i]);
    }
}
```

Next, compile the C code to create a shared library (**.so** file on Linux).

```
gcc -shared -fPIC -o libcustom_math.so custom_math.c
```

Next, load the C library in Python using **ctypes**:

```
import ctypes
import numpy as np
# Load the shared library
lib = ctypes.CDLL('./libcustom_math.so')
# Define the argument and return types of the function
lib.custom_exp.argtypes = [
    ctypes.c_int,
    np.ctypeslib.ndpointer(dtype=np.float64, ndim=1,
flags='C_CONTIGUOUS'),
    np.ctypeslib.ndpointer(dtype=np.float64, ndim=1,
flags='C_CONTIGUOUS')
]
lib.custom_exp.restype = None
```

Define Wrapper Function in Python

We need to create a Python function that wraps the C function.

```
def custom_exp_c(x):

    x_np = np.ascontiguousarray(x, dtype=np.float64)

    y_np = np.empty_like(x_np)

    n = x_np.size

    lib.custom_exp(n, x_np, y_np)

    return y_np
```

Integrate with JAX using 'jax.experimental.callback'

Since JAX does not natively support calling arbitrary Python functions within JIT-compiled code, you can use **`jax.experimental.callback`** (available in JAX versions >= 0.2.12).

```
import jax

from jax.experimental import callback as jec

@jax.custom_vjp

def custom_exp(x):

    def forward(x):

        y = jec.call(custom_exp_c, x,
output_shape=x.shape)

        return y

    def backward(res, g):

        return (g * custom_exp(x),)

    return forward(x), backward

# Define the forward and backward passes
```

```
def custom_exp_fwd(x):
    y = jec.call(custom_exp_c, x, output_shape=x.shape)
    return y, y  # Return y as residual for backward
def custom_exp_bwd(res, g):
    y = res
    return (g * y,)  # Derivative of exp(x) is exp(x)
custom_exp.defvjp(custom_exp_fwd, custom_exp_bwd)
```

Next, test the custom function:

```
import jax.numpy as jnp
# Sample input
x = jnp.array([0.0, 1.0, 2.0], dtype=jnp.float64)
# Call the custom_exp function
y = custom_exp(x)
print("y =", y)
# Compute the gradient
grad_fn = jax.grad(lambda x: jnp.sum(custom_exp(x)))
grad_value = grad_fn(x)
print("grad_value =", grad_value)
```

Next, use the function with JIT compilation:

```
@jax.jit
def compute_custom_exp(x):
```

```
    return custom_exp(x)

y_jit = compute_custom_exp(x)

print("y_jit =", y_jit)
```

Here, the use of **jax.experimental.callback** may introduce performance overhead due to data transfer between the device and host. The external function is executed on the CPU, which may not be optimal if the rest of your computation is on the GPU.

Handling Data Types and Shapes

Just make sure that the data types and shapes are compatible between JAX and the C function. Just use **np.ascontiguousarray** to make sure the memory is contiguous. Make sure you match up the data types (e.g., np.float64 in both JAX and C).

Next, You can now use **custom_exp**.

```
def model(x):

    return custom_exp(x) + x

# Compute gradient

grad_model = jax.grad(lambda x: jnp.sum(model(x)))

grad_value = grad_model(x)

print("Model grad_value =", grad_value)
```

You can use JAX's FFI capabilities and **jax.experimental.callback** to integrate external C libraries into your JAX computations. This approach lets you use optimized C code in your models, which can extend functionality and potentially improve performance. There are some limits to how well this works on GPUs and there might be some overhead, but it's a pretty good way of connecting C code with JAX.

Performance Optimization with Custom CUDA Kernels

When it comes to high-performance computing tasks using GPUs, the standard operations provided by JAX might not be as efficient as you need for specific computations. You might need to create your own algorithms or tweak certain operations to get better results than what JAX's library offers. Writing your own CUDA kernels lets you tweak computations to get the best performance on GPUs. The tricky part is figuring out how to integrate these custom kernels with JAX. We need to make sure they work together seamlessly with JAX's JIT compilation and automatic differentiation.

JAX lets you integrate custom CUDA kernels using custom calls in XLA. If you define a custom JAX primitive and provide GPU-specific translations, you can write a custom CUDA kernel, compile it, and register it with JAX's backend. This integration lets you use the custom kernel in JAX computations, getting the best of both worlds—the performance of the custom kernel and JAX's features.

Write Custom CUDA Kernel

First, you'll want to create a CUDA kernel for the operation you want to optimize. For instance, you could implement a custom element-wise multiplication.

```
// custom_mul.cu

extern "C" __global__ void custom_mul_kernel(const float* x, const float* y, float* out, int n) {

    int idx = blockIdx.x * blockDim.x + threadIdx.x;

    if (idx < n) {

        out[idx] = x[idx] * y[idx];

    }

}
```

Compile CUDA Kernel to PTX

Next, you'll want to compile the CUDA kernel to generate PTX code, which you can then load with JAX.

```
nvcc --ptx custom_mul.cu -o custom_mul.ptx
```

Load PTX Code in Python

Just read the PTX code into Python for registration.

```
with open('custom_mul.ptx', 'r') as f:

    ptx_code = f.read()
```

Define Custom JAX Primitive

We need to create a custom primitive for the multiplication operation.

```
from jax import core

from jax.interpreters import xla

custom_mul_p = core.Primitive('custom_mul')

def custom_mul_abstract(x, y):

    return core.ShapedArray(x.shape, x.dtype)

custom_mul_p.def_abstract_eval(custom_mul_abstract)
```

You maay define how the primitive behaves when running on the CPU.

```
def custom_mul_impl(x, y):

    return x * y

custom_mul_p.def_impl(custom_mul_impl)
```

Register Custom Call Target

Next, register the custom CUDA kernel with XLA.

```
from jax.lib import xla_client

def register_custom_call():

    xla_client.register_custom_call_target(
```

```
        b'custom_mul_kernel',
        ptx_code.encode('utf-8'),
        platform='CUDA',
    )
register_custom_call()
```

Define GPU Translation

Next, please provide the GPU translation for the custom primitive.

```
def custom_mul_xla_translation_gpu(c, x, y):
    shape = c.get_shape(x)
    dtype = shape.element_type()
    n = shape.dimensions()[0]
    out_shape = xla_client.Shape.array_shape(dtype, [n])
    n_const = xla_client.ops.Constant(c, np.array(n,
dtype=np.int32))
    return xla_client.ops.CustomCall(
        c,
        b'custom_mul_kernel',
        operands=(x, y, n_const),
        shape=out_shape
    )
```

```
xla.backend_specific_translations['gpu'][custom_mul_p] =
custom_mul_xla_translation_gpu
```

Define Forward Function and JVP Rule

We need to write a function using the custom primitive.

```
def custom_mul(x, y):

    return custom_mul_p.bind(x, y)
```

Just give us the Jacobian-vector product rule so we can do the automatic differentiation.

```
from jax.interpreters import ad

def custom_mul_jvp(primals, tangents):

    x, y = primals

    x_dot, y_dot = tangents

    primal_out = custom_mul(x, y)

    tangent_out = x_dot * y + x * y_dot

    return primal_out, tangent_out

ad.defjvp(custom_mul_p, custom_mul_jvp)
```

Verify GPU Execution

Next, ensure that the computation is executed on the GPU.

```
from jax.lib import xla_bridge

backend = xla_bridge.get_backend()

assert backend.platform == 'gpu', "Not running on GPU"

# Move data to GPU explicitly
```

```
x_gpu = jax.device_put(x)

y_gpu = jax.device_put(y)

result_gpu = compute_custom_mul(x_gpu, y_gpu)

print("Result on GPU:", result_gpu)
```

Optimize CUDA Kernel

Make your kernel work better for you:

- It's important to choose the right block and grid sizes.
- If it's helpful, use shared memory.
- It's best to minimize memory accesses and optimize memory patterns.

Following is a quick example with kernel launch parameters:

```
def custom_mul_xla_translation_gpu(c, x, y):

    # Previous code...

    # Define launch dimensions

    launch_dims = xla_client.ops.Constant(c,
np.array([n], dtype=np.int32))

    # Pass launch dimensions in backend_config

    backend_config =
xla_client._xla_ops.BuildGpuLaunchConfig(launch_dims)

    return xla_client.ops.CustomCall(

        c,

        b'custom_mul_kernel',

        operands=(x, y, n_const),

        shape=out_shape,
```

```
        backend_config=backend_config
    )
```

If you define your own primitives and provide GPU-specific translations, you can use the power of custom kernels while getting the benefits of JAX's automatic differentiation and JIT compilation. This approach needs to be done right and you need to understand both CUDA programming and JAX's internal mechanisms, but it can lead to big performance gains for specialised operations.

Handling Data Conversion between JAX and External Code

When you're integrating JAX with external code or foreign functions, you'll often run into data format mismatches. These mismatches can happen because the data types, memory layouts, or dimensionality of JAX arrays don't match what external libraries expect. These differences can cause problems, like errors, incorrect calculations, or slow data processing. The tricky part is creating solid data conversion routines that make sure JAX and external code work well together, keeping data safe and making sure the whole integration process is efficient.

To make data conversion between JAX and external code work well, you need to set up some systematic data transformation routines that deal with differences in data types, memory layouts, and array dimensions.

The main steps are:

1. Understand the data types and structures expected by both JAX and the external code.
2. Convert data types to match the requirements of the target environment.
3. Adjust memory layouts (e.g., C-contiguous vs. Fortran-contiguous) to meet the expectations of external libraries.
4. Modify array shapes or dimensions as needed to align with external function interfaces.
5. Create reusable functions or utilities to streamline the conversion process across different parts of your codebase.

If you take the time to get these things right, you can build a solid connection between JAX and external code, making it easier and more efficient to share data.

Understand Data Formats

Now, before implementing data conversion routines, it is essential to comprehend the data formats used by both JAX and the external code. For instance, JAX primarily uses **jax.numpy** arrays, which are similar to NumPy arrays, while external libraries might expect raw C arrays, specific memory alignments, or different data types.

Let's say you have a JAX array that you need to pass to a C library function that's expecting a C-style contiguous array of float32 values. Figure out exactly what data types the external code is looking for. If you don't match up the data types, you might end up with the wrong results or run into problems when the code runs.

The case may be that the external C function expects data in **float32** format, whereas your JAX array might be in **float64** format.

Implement Explicit Type Casting

Just use JAX's type casting functions and you'll be able to convert your data to the required type. JAX has got you covered with functions like **astype** to make this process a breeze.

```
import jax.numpy as jnp

# Original JAX array in float64

jax_array = jnp.array([1.0, 2.0, 3.0], dtype=jnp.float64)

# Convert to float32

jax_array_float32 = jax_array.astype(jnp.float32)
```

Ensure Memory Layout Compatibility

Sometimes, external libraries need data to be laid out a certain way in memory, like C-contiguous (row-major) or Fortran-contiguous (column-major). JAX arrays are usually C-contiguous, but it's a good idea to check and make sure the layout is correct.

If the external library expects C-contiguous arrays, then ensure that the JAX array meets this requirement.

```
# Ensure the array is C-contiguous

if not jax_array_float32.flags['C_CONTIGUOUS']:

    jax_array_float32 =
jnp.ascontiguousarray(jax_array_float32)
```

Handle Array Dimensionality

Next, make sure that the dimensions of the array align with the expectations of the external function. This might involve reshaping or expanding dimensions.

If the C function expects a 1D array but your JAX array is 2D, reshape it accordingly.

```
# Original JAX array shape: (3, 1)

jax_array_2d = jnp.array([[1.0], [2.0], [3.0]],
dtype=jnp.float32)

# Reshape to 1D array

jax_array_1d = jax_array_2d.reshape(-1)
```

Convert JAX Arrays to NumPy for External Libraries

The great thing about NumPy is that most external C libraries work really well with it. Before you pass the JAX arrays to the external functions, you'll want to convert them to NumPy arrays.

```
# Convert JAX array to NumPy array

numpy_array = jax_array_float32.device_buffer.to_py()
```

Alternatively, we can use **`np.asarray`** to create a NumPy view:

```
import numpy as np

# Create a NumPy view without copying

numpy_array = np.asarray(jax_array_float32)
```

Implement Data Conversion Functions

Let's come up with some reusable functions to streamline the conversion process. That'll make things more consistent and cut out a lot of the repetition.

```
def jax_to_c_array(jax_array, dtype=jnp.float32, ndim=1):
```

```
    """
    Converts a JAX array to a C-compatible NumPy array.

    Parameters:
    - jax_array: jax.numpy array
    - dtype: desired data type (default: float32)
    - ndim: desired number of dimensions (default: 1)

    Returns:
    - NumPy array with specified dtype and dimensions
    """
    # Cast to desired dtype
    array_cast = jax_array.astype(dtype)

    # Ensure C-contiguous
    if not array_cast.flags['C_CONTIGUOUS']:
        array_cast = jnp.ascontiguousarray(array_cast)

    # Reshape if necessary
    if array_cast.ndim != ndim:
        array_cast = array_cast.reshape((-1,) if ndim ==
1 else array_cast.shape)
```

```
    # Convert to NumPy
    numpy_array = np.asarray(array_cast)

    return numpy_array
```

Integrate with External C Functions using 'ctypes'

You can use Python's **ctypes** library to connect with those external C functions. Just pass the converted NumPy arrays as pointers. For example, assume you have the following C function compiled into a shared library (**libcustom_math.so**):

```
// custom_math.c
#include <math.h>
void custom_exp(int n, const float* x, float* y) {
    for (int i = 0; i < n; ++i) {
        y[i] = expf(x[i]);
    }
}
```

Next, load the shared library and define argument types.

```
import ctypes
# Load the shared library
lib = ctypes.CDLL('./libcustom_math.so')
# Define the argument and return types
```

```
lib.custom_exp.argtypes = [
    ctypes.c_int,
    ctypes.POINTER(ctypes.c_float),
    ctypes.POINTER(ctypes.c_float)
]
lib.custom_exp.restype = None
```

Then, create a Python function that wraps the C function, handling data conversion internally.

```
def custom_exp_jax(x):
    """
    Applies the custom C exponential function to a JAX
array.

    Parameters:
    - x: jax.numpy array

    Returns:
    - y: jax.numpy array after applying exp
    """
    # Convert JAX array to C-compatible NumPy array
    x_c = jax_to_c_array(x, dtype=jnp.float32, ndim=1)
    n = x_c.size
```

```
    # Prepare output array
    y_c = np.empty_like(x_c)

    # Get pointers to the data
    x_ptr =
x_c.ctypes.data_as(ctypes.POINTER(ctypes.c_float))
    y_ptr =
y_c.ctypes.data_as(ctypes.POINTER(ctypes.c_float))

    # Call the C function
    lib.custom_exp(n, x_ptr, y_ptr)

    # Convert the result back to JAX array
    y_jax = jnp.array(y_c)

    return y_jax
```

Integrate with JAX's JIT Compilation

To maintain JAX's performance benefits, especially JIT compilation, you can wrap the external function appropriately. However, JAX's JIT cannot compile Python functions that involve **`ctypes`** calls. To work around this, you can use **`jax.custom_jvp`** or **`jax.experimental.callback`**, though these methods have limitations.

```
from jax.experimental import callback as jec
```

```
@jax.custom_vjp
def custom_exp(x):
    return custom_exp_jax(x)
# Define the forward and backward passes
def custom_exp_fwd(x):
    y = custom_exp_jax(x)
    return y, y  # Return y as residual for backward
def custom_exp_bwd(res, g):
    # The derivative of exp is exp, so gradient is g * y
    y, = res
    return (g * y,)
custom_exp.defvjp(custom_exp_fwd, custom_exp_bwd)
```

Optimize Data Conversion Performance

Data conversion can add some extra steps, especially with larger datasets. To get around this, think about trying out these strategies:

- Use views or in-place operations where possible to avoid unnecessary data duplication. For example, use **np.asarray** to create a view without copying.

```
numpy_array = np.asarray(jax_array_float32)
```

- Convert data in batches to leverage vectorized operations and reduce per-element processing overhead.
- For frequent data transfers between JAX and external code, pin memory to accelerate data movement.

Following is a quick example using NumPy's **memmap**:

```
# Create a memory-mapped file

mmap_file = np.memmap('data.dat', dtype='float32',
mode='w+', shape=(1000,))

# Use memmap for data exchange

mmap_file[:] = jax_array_float32
```

After conversion, ensure that the data remains accurate and consistent.

Once you know the ins and outs of the data formats, how explicit type casting works, and how to automate conversion routines, you can create a rock-solid interface between JAX and external libraries. It's also important to make sure data is valid and manage multidimensional arrays properly for accurate computations.

Managing Thread Safety and Concurrency

When integrating JAX with external functions or foreign code, especially in multi-threaded environments, concurrency issues such as race conditions, deadlocks, and data corruption can arise. External libraries not designed with thread safety in mind may inadvertently cause these issues when accessed concurrently. Managing thread safety and ensuring proper concurrency control is essential to maintain the integrity and reliability of your computations. The challenge lies in implementing strategies that prevent concurrent access problems while allowing efficient parallel execution, especially when leveraging JAX's parallelism features alongside external code.

To manage thread safety and concurrency when using FFI with JAX, you can adopt several best practices and strategies:

1. Familiarize yourself with how both JAX and the external libraries handle threading.
2. Prefer libraries that are designed to be thread-safe or provide mechanisms to ensure safe concurrent access.
3. Use threading locks (e.g., mutexes) to serialize access to non-thread-safe external functions.
4. When using JAX's parallelization features (**pmap**, **vmap**), ensure that external function calls within these mappings are thread-safe.
5. Reduce reliance on shared mutable state between threads to prevent race conditions.
6. Rigorously test your integrated system under concurrent access to identify and resolve potential issues.

If you use these strategies, you can easily manage thread safety and concurrency. This means your JAX models will be able to work well with external functions in multi-threaded environments.

Assess and Choose Thread Safety of External Libraries

Let's say you're integrating with an external C library for image processing. Take a look at the library's documentation to see if its functions are safe to call from multiple threads at the same time. Take a look at the library documentation or source code to see what it says about concurrency.

It's best to pick external libraries that are already thread-safe, or ones that can make sure they're thread-safe. In fact, many modern libraries are designed with thread safety in mind, offering thread-safe APIs or internal synchronization.

Implement Synchronization Mechanisms

If you're using external libraries that aren't thread-safe, you'll need to implement some kind of synchronization mechanism to serialize access and prevent concurrent execution issues.

```
import threading

import ctypes

import jax.numpy as jnp

# Load the external C library

lib = ctypes.CDLL('./libcustom_math.so')

# Define the function signature

lib.custom_exp.argtypes = [

    ctypes.c_int,

    ctypes.POINTER(ctypes.c_float),

    ctypes.POINTER(ctypes.c_float)

]

lib.custom_exp.restype = None
```

```
# Initialize a lock
custom_exp_lock = threading.Lock()
def custom_exp_thread_safe(x):
    with custom_exp_lock:
        # Convert JAX array to NumPy array
        x_np = jax_to_c_array(x, dtype=jnp.float32,
ndim=1)
        n = x_np.size
        y_np = jnp.empty_like(x_np)

        # Get pointers
        x_ptr =
x_np.ctypes.data_as(ctypes.POINTER(ctypes.c_float))
        y_ptr =
y_np.ctypes.data_as(ctypes.POINTER(ctypes.c_float))

        # Call the external C function
        lib.custom_exp(n, x_ptr, y_ptr)

        # Convert back to JAX array
        y_jax = jnp.array(y_np)
    return y_jax
```

Wrap External Functions with Thread-safe Interfaces

Next, put together wrapper functions to handle synchronization, making sure to keep external function calls in sequence.

Following is an example using Decorators:

```
from functools import wraps

def thread_safe(func):

    @wraps(func)

    def wrapper(*args, **kwargs):

        with custom_exp_lock:

            return func(*args, **kwargs)

    return wrapper

@thread_safe

def custom_exp_safe(x):

    # Conversion and external call

    x_np = jax_to_c_array(x, dtype=jnp.float32, ndim=1)

    n = x_np.size

    y_np = jnp.empty_like(x_np)

    x_ptr =
x_np.ctypes.data_as(ctypes.POINTER(ctypes.c_float))

    y_ptr =
y_np.ctypes.data_as(ctypes.POINTER(ctypes.c_float))

    lib.custom_exp(n, x_ptr, y_ptr)

    y_jax = jnp.array(y_np)
```

```
    return y_jax
```

Integrate with JAX's JIT Compilation

If you're using JIT compilation, it's important to make sure that thread safety is maintained. Because the code is running in parallel, you should avoid putting locks inside the compiled code. Instead, handle synchronization outside of the JIT functions.

```
@jax.jit

def jitted_custom_exp(x):

    # JIT-compiled function should not contain locks

    return custom_exp_safe(x)  # Ensure custom_exp_safe
handles locking
```

While using parallel mapping functions, ensure that external function calls within mapped functions are thread-safe or appropriately synchronized.

```
# Define a parallel mapped function

parallel_custom_exp = jax.pmap(custom_exp_safe)

# Sample input batch

x_batch = jnp.array([

    [1.0, 2.0, 3.0],

    [4.0, 5.0, 6.0],

    [7.0, 8.0, 9.0],

    [10.0, 11.0, 12.0]

], dtype=jnp.float32)

# Apply the parallel custom exponential
```

```
y_batch = parallel_custom_exp(x_batch)
print("y_batch =", y_batch)
```

Minimize Shared State

It's best to avoid using the same shared data between different threads. This can help to prevent race conditions and data corruption. Wherever you can, make sure each thread is working with its own data.

```
def custom_exp_isolated(x):
    # No shared state modification
    return custom_exp_safe(x)
```

For managing multiple threads efficiently, use thread pools or executors provided by Python's **concurrent.futures** module. This allows better control over thread lifecycle and resource management.

```
from concurrent.futures import ThreadPoolExecutor
# Initialize a thread pool
executor = ThreadPoolExecutor(max_workers=4)
# Define a function to submit tasks
def submit_custom_exp_tasks(inputs):
    futures = [executor.submit(custom_exp_safe, x) for x
in inputs]
    results = [future.result() for future in futures]
    return jnp.stack(results)
# Sample inputs
inputs = [jnp.array([1.0, 2.0, 3.0], dtype=jnp.float32),
```

```
        jnp.array([4.0, 5.0, 6.0], dtype=jnp.float32),
        jnp.array([7.0, 8.0, 9.0], dtype=jnp.float32),
        jnp.array([10.0, 11.0, 12.0],
dtype=jnp.float32)]
# Submit tasks and get results
y_results = submit_custom_exp_tasks(inputs)
print("y_results =", y_results)
```

Use Asynchronous Programming for Non-blocking Calls

For I/O-bound external functions, try consider using asynchronous programming to prevent blocking the main thread, improving overall performance.

Following is a quick example using **asyncio**:

```
import asyncio
async def async_custom_exp(x):
    return custom_exp_safe(x)
async def main_async():
    inputs = [jnp.array([1.0, 2.0, 3.0],
dtype=jnp.float32),
              jnp.array([4.0, 5.0, 6.0],
dtype=jnp.float32)]
    tasks = [async_custom_exp(x) for x in inputs]
    results = await asyncio.gather(*tasks)
    return jnp.stack(results)
# Run the asynchronous main function
```

```
y_async = asyncio.run(main_async())

print("y_async =", y_async)
```

Implement Read-Write Locks for Granular Control

If certain external functions allow concurrent reads but require exclusive access for writes, implement read-write locks to optimize concurrency.

```
class ReadWriteLock:

    def __init__(self):

        self.lock = threading.RLock()

        self.readers = 0


    def acquire_read(self):

        with self.lock:

            self.readers += 1


    def release_read(self):

        with self.lock:

            self.readers -= 1


    def acquire_write(self):

        self.lock.acquire()

        while self.readers > 0:
```

```
            pass  # Busy wait or implement condition
variables


    def release_write(self):

        self.lock.release()

# Initialize the read-write lock

rw_lock = ReadWriteLock()

def custom_exp_rw(x):

    rw_lock.acquire_write()

    try:

        return custom_exp_safe(x)

    finally:

        rw_lock.release_write()
```

It's really important to think about thread safety and concurrency when you're integrating JAX with external functions. This helps to make sure that everything runs smoothly and efficiently. If you understand JAX's threading model, assess the thread safety of external libraries, implement appropriate synchronization mechanisms, and integrate with JAX's parallel execution features in the right way, you can avoid concurrency issues like race conditions and deadlocks. On top of that, if you keep the shared state to a minimum, use thread pools, and do asynchronous programming when it makes sense, you can get better performance without any loss of safety.

Distributing Computations across Heterogeneous Systems

In advanced machine learning projects, there is often a need to leverage specialized hardware such as FPGAs (Field-Programmable Gate Arrays) or ASICs (Application-Specific Integrated Circuits) to perform specific computations more efficiently than general-purpose GPUs or CPUs. These specialized devices can offer significant speedups and energy efficiency for tasks they are optimized for. However, integrating these heterogeneous systems with JAX poses challenges, including managing data transfer, ensuring compatibility, and orchestrating computation across different hardware platforms. The challenge lies in effectively utilizing JAX's FFI capabilities to offload computations to these specialized devices, thereby enhancing overall system performance without compromising on ease of use or flexibility.

Now, to distribute computations across heterogeneous systems using JAX's FFI, we can follow a structured approach:

1. Determine which parts of the model or computations would benefit most from acceleration by specialized hardware.
2. Use or create interfaces that allow communication between JAX and the specialized hardware, often through custom APIs or drivers.
3. Efficiently manage the transfer of data between JAX (typically running on CPUs or GPUs) and the specialized devices.
4. Use FFI tools like **`ctypes`**, **`cffi`**, or JAX's custom primitives to call functions running on specialized hardware.
5. Manage synchronization between different hardware operations and ensure data type and memory layout compatibility.
6. Fine-tune the data transfer and computation processes to minimize latency and maximize throughput.

If we pay close attention to each step, we can build a solid system where JAX can offload certain calculations to specialised hardware. This lets us use their unique features to improve overall performance.

Identify Computation-intensive Tasks

So first, begin by profiling your JAX model to identify bottlenecks or operations that are computationally intensive and could benefit from hardware acceleration. Common candidates include matrix multiplications, convolutions, or custom operations that involve large-scale data processing.

For example, suppose a custom activation function or a large matrix multiplication in your model is identified as a performance bottleneck.

Choose appropriate Specialized Hardware

Select the specialized hardware that best suits the identified tasks. For instance:

- FPGAs are highly configurable and excel at parallel processing tasks with low latency.
- ASICs offer optimized performance for specific applications with high efficiency.

If existing interfaces or libraries are available for your chosen hardware, leverage them. Otherwise, you may need to develop custom drivers or APIs to communicate with the hardware. For an FPGA, you might use OpenCL or a vendor-specific SDK to program and communicate with the device.

Implement Data Transfer Mechanisms

Efficient data transfer between JAX and the specialized hardware is crucial. This involves converting JAX arrays to the format expected by the hardware and managing the memory layout. Check the below example using **ctypes**:

```
import ctypes

import numpy as np

import jax.numpy as jnp

# Load the shared library for FPGA operations

fpga_lib = ctypes.CDLL('./libfpga_ops.so')

# Define the function signature

fpga_lib.custom_matmul.argtypes = [

    ctypes.c_int,

    ctypes.POINTER(ctypes.c_float),

    ctypes.POINTER(ctypes.c_float),

    ctypes.POINTER(ctypes.c_float)

]

fpga_lib.custom_matmul.restype = None

def custom_matmul_fpga(a, b):

    # Ensure input arrays are float32 and C-contiguous
```

```
    a_np = np.ascontiguousarray(np.asarray(a,
dtype=np.float32))
    b_np = np.ascontiguousarray(np.asarray(b,
dtype=np.float32))
    n = a_np.shape[0]
    m = b_np.shape[1]
    k = a_np.shape[1]

    # Prepare output array
    c_np = np.empty((n, m), dtype=np.float32)

    # Get pointers to the data
    a_ptr =
a_np.ctypes.data_as(ctypes.POINTER(ctypes.c_float))
    b_ptr =
b_np.ctypes.data_as(ctypes.POINTER(ctypes.c_float))
    c_ptr =
c_np.ctypes.data_as(ctypes.POINTER(ctypes.c_float))

    # Call the FPGA function
    fpga_lib.custom_matmul(n, a_ptr, b_ptr, c_ptr)

    # Convert back to JAX array
```

```
    return jnp.array(c_np)
```

Integrate with JAX using Custom Primitives

To keep everything working together smoothly, wrap the FPGA function as a custom JAX primitive. That way, you can maintain compatibility with JAX's JIT compilation and automatic differentiation.

```
from jax import core

from jax.interpreters import xla

# Define the primitive

custom_matmul_p = core.Primitive('custom_matmul_fpga')

# Define the abstract evaluation

def custom_matmul_abstract(x, y):

    return core.ShapedArray((x.shape[0], y.shape[1]),
x.dtype)

custom_matmul_p.def_abstract_eval(custom_matmul_abstract)

# Define the implementation

def custom_matmul_impl(x, y):

    return custom_matmul_fpga(x, y)

custom_matmul_p.def_impl(custom_matmul_impl)

# Define the XLA translation for CPU (optional)

def custom_matmul_cpu_translation(c, x, y):

    # Implement CPU fallback or raise NotImplementedError

    raise NotImplementedError("custom_matmul_fpga is only
implemented for FPGA.")
```

```
xla.backend_specific_translations['cpu'][custom_matmul_p]
= custom_matmul_cpu_translation

# Define the JVP rule for differentiation

from jax.interpreters import ad

def custom_matmul_jvp(primals, tangents):

    x, y = primals

    x_dot, y_dot = tangents

    primal_out = custom_matmul_p.bind(x, y)

    tangent_out = jnp.dot(x_dot, y) + jnp.dot(x, y_dot)

    return primal_out, tangent_out

ad.defjvp(custom_matmul_p, custom_matmul_jvp)
```

Define User-friendly Function

Let's create a high-level function that users can call easily within their JAX code.

```
def custom_matmul(x, y):

    return custom_matmul_p.bind(x, y)
```

Now, ensure that the custom primitive works correctly within JAX computations.

```
import jax.numpy as jnp

# Sample inputs

a = jnp.array([[1.0, 2.0], [3.0, 4.0]],
dtype=jnp.float32)

b = jnp.array([[5.0, 6.0], [7.0, 8.0]],
dtype=jnp.float32)
```

```
# Perform matrix multiplication using FPGA

c = custom_matmul(a, b)

print("Result from FPGA:", c)

# Compute gradients

grad_fn = jax.grad(lambda a, b: jnp.sum(custom_matmul(a, b)))

grad_a, grad_b = grad_fn(a, b)

print("Gradients:", grad_a, grad_b)
```

Aim for less overhead in data transfer by batching operations or reusing memory buffers whenever you can. For example, if performing multiple matrix multiplications, reuse allocated memory to avoid repeated allocations and transfers.

```
def batched_custom_matmul(batch_a, batch_b):

    # Assuming batch_a and batch_b are batched arrays

    return jax.vmap(custom_matmul)(batch_a, batch_b)
```

Handle Specialized Data Types

If the specialized hardware requires unique data types, implement necessary conversions within the data transfer routines. For example, if FPGA requires fixed-point representation:

```
def float_to_fixed(x, scale=1000):

    return jnp.round(x * scale).astype(jnp.int32)

def fixed_to_float(x, scale=1000):

    return x.astype(jnp.float32) / scale

def custom_matmul_fpga_fixed(a, b):
```

```
    a_fixed = float_to_fixed(a)

    b_fixed = float_to_fixed(b)

    c_fixed = custom_matmul_fpga(a_fixed, b_fixed)

    return fixed_to_float(c_fixed)
```

Make sure you coordinate your calculations across different hardware to avoid any issues with data consistency or inconsistencies. Either use synchronization primitives or make sure that data transfers are finished before starting dependent computations.

```
def synchronized_custom_matmul(x, y):

    with custom_sync_lock:

        return custom_matmul(x, y)
```

Handle Errors and Exceptions

As we've seen before, it's important to have a solid plan in place for when the external hardware doesn't work as it should or gives us unexpected results.

```
def safe_custom_matmul(x, y):

    try:

        return custom_matmul(x, y)

    except Exception as e:

        print("Error during custom_matmul:", e)

        return jnp.dot(x, y)  # Fallback to standard JAX
operation
```

By following these steps, you successfully distributed computations across heterogeneous systems using JAX's FFI capabilities. Offloading specific tasks to specialized hardware like FPGAs or ASICs allowed for significant performance enhancements tailored to your project's needs. This integration involved careful data conversion, defining custom JAX primitives, managing synchronization, and ensuring compatibility with JAX's compilation and differentiation mechanisms.

Summary

Overall, we successfully enhanced the flexibility and performance of our machine learning models by investigating and integrating foreign functions within JAX. First, we successfully addressed the challenge of calling external C libraries from JAX. We were able to wrap C functions and integrate them as custom primitives. This allowed us to leverage optimized C code within JAX's computation graph, expanding our model's capabilities. Next, we optimized performance by writing custom CUDA kernels, allowing us to execute specific operations more efficiently on GPUs. We defined custom primitives, compiled CUDA code, and ensured seamless integration with JAX's JIT compilation and automatic differentiation mechanisms.

We also made it a priority to handle data conversion between JAX and external code. To do this, we implemented robust routines that manage differences in data types, memory layouts, and array dimensions. This guaranteed compatibility and maintained data integrity during interactions with foreign functions. We also solved thread safety and concurrency issues using synchronization mechanisms and best practices, eliminating race conditions and guaranteeing reliable computations in multi-threaded environments. Finally, we explored distributing computations across heterogeneous systems, utilizing FFI to offload tasks to specialized hardware like FPGAs and ASICs. This integration not only optimized performance, but also demonstrated the scalability of our models across diverse hardware platforms. Overall, the chapter provided us with the necessary strategies and technical knowledge to effectively integrate external code with JAX, significantly enhancing the functionality and efficiency of our machine learning projects.

CHAPTER 8: TRAINING NEURAL NETWORKS WITH JAX

Overview

In this chapter, we will master the art of training neural networks, including practical techniques for building and optimizing models effectively. We start by learning how to load data efficiently using TensorFlow Datasets, which makes data preparation for large-scale machine learning tasks simple. This simple yet effective recipe ensures smooth data feeding into the training pipeline, enabling faster and more efficient training.

Next, we'll construct a neural network from scratch using JAX. You'll learn to design and implement custom architectures tailored to specific tasks. Then, we'll use Penzai for experiment tracking during training. This tool manages experiments by tracking metrics, hyperparameters, and results. It makes it easier to evaluate model performance. Lastly, we'll cover techniques for evaluating and visualizing model performance. You'll gain insights into model accuracy and training dynamics. You'll also learn how to refine and debug models.

Efficient Data Loading with TensorFlow Datasets

Data loading often becomes a bottleneck in training pipelines, especially when dealing with large datasets. Slow data loading can significantly hinder the training process, leading to inefficient GPU utilization and increased training times. To address this issue, we need a practical solution to efficiently load large datasets, pre-process them on-the-fly, and feed them to the training loop. In this recipe, we will use TensorFlow Datasets for seamless data loading and preprocessing, allowing us to integrate the data pipeline with JAX for training our neural network.

This recipe will guide you through the process of setting up TFDS to efficiently load and prepare data for training a neural network using JAX, leveraging TensorFlow's optimized data handling capabilities. This approach will enable us to load large datasets, apply necessary transformations, and seamlessly integrate the processed data with JAX.

Following are the steps:

1. Setting up TensorFlow Datasets and selecting a suitable dataset.
2. Configuring the data pipeline for efficient loading, shuffling, and batching.
3. Converting the TensorFlow data format to a JAX-compatible format.
4. Integrating the data loader into the JAX training pipeline.

Loading Dataset using TFDS

First, ensure that TensorFlow is available in your environment. Since we have TensorFlow already installed, we can import TensorFlow Datasets. Next, load the dataset from TFDS and configure it for training and evaluation.

Here, we will split the data into training and testing sets.

```
# Load the Fashion MNIST dataset

dataset_name = 'fashion_mnist'

(train_ds, test_ds), ds_info = tfds.load(

    dataset_name,

    split=['train', 'test'],

    as_supervised=True,  # This returns (image, label)
pairs

    with_info=True

)

# Print dataset information

print(ds_info)
```

Preprocessing Data

Now, to train the model effectively, we need to preprocess the data. This includes normalizing the pixel values to the range **[0, 1]**, shuffling, batching, and optionally applying data augmentation.

```
def preprocess(image, label):

    # Normalize the images to [0, 1]

    image = tf.cast(image, tf.float32) / 255.0

    return image, label

# Batch size for training

batch_size = 128
```

```
# Configure the training dataset pipeline

train_ds = (train_ds

            .map(preprocess,
num_parallel_calls=tf.data.AUTOTUNE)

            .shuffle(buffer_size=10000)

            .batch(batch_size)

            .prefetch(buffer_size=tf.data.AUTOTUNE))

# Configure the testing dataset pipeline

test_ds = (test_ds

           .map(preprocess,
num_parallel_calls=tf.data.AUTOTUNE)

           .batch(batch_size)

           .prefetch(buffer_size=tf.data.AUTOTUNE))
```

Here, we use **tf.data.AUTOTUNE** to automatically optimize the parallelism of data loading, which helps in speeding up the data pipeline. The **.shuffle()** method randomizes the order of examples, while **.batch()** groups the examples into batches for efficient training.

Converting TensorFlow Data to JAX-compatible Format

To use the data with JAX, we need to convert the TensorFlow dataset format to NumPy arrays that can be processed by JAX functions. We will use the **tfds.as_numpy()** utility to convert the dataset into an iterable that provides JAX-compatible NumPy arrays.

```
# Convert TensorFlow datasets to JAX-compatible format

train_ds = tfds.as_numpy(train_ds)

test_ds = tfds.as_numpy(test_ds)
```

Now, **train_ds** and **test_ds** are iterables that provide batches of data in the form of NumPy arrays, which are compatible with JAX.

Integrating Data Loader with JAX Training Loop

Next, to integrate the data loader with the JAX training pipeline, we will write a training loop that fetches batches of data from the preprocessed dataset and feeds them into a model for training.

```
# Example function to simulate a training step

def train_step(params, images, labels):

    # A placeholder function to demonstrate using the
data

    # In actual implementation, this would involve
computing loss and updating parameters

    logits = jax.nn.relu(jnp.dot(images, params['w']) +
params['b'])

    loss = jnp.mean((logits - labels) ** 2)

    return loss

# Simulating a training process

def train_model(train_ds, params, num_epochs=5):

    for epoch in range(num_epochs):

        epoch_loss = 0

        for batch in train_ds:

            images, labels = batch

            # Perform the training step

            batch_loss = train_step(params, images,
labels)
```

```
            epoch_loss += batch_loss

        print(f"Epoch {epoch + 1}, Loss: {epoch_loss}")
```

This example demonstrates a simple training loop that processes data in batches. The **train_step** function performs operations on the data using JAX.

By using TensorFlow Datasets for data loading, preprocessing, and augmentation, we were able to fix the data loading bottleneck and integrate with JAX without a hitch. This way, we make sure large datasets are handled smoothly, use all our hardware resources like GPUs as much as we can, and get faster training.

Building Neural Network from Scratch

Think of a situation where we have to build a custom neural network from scratch with JAX, without using high-level libraries like Flax or Haiku. Building a neural network like this helps us understand how it works, which gives us more control over the architecture and the training process. This recipe will show you how to build a fully connected neural network, set its parameters, do the forward pass, compute the loss, and integrate it with our Fashion MNIST dataset.

To build a neural network in JAX, we just need to follow these steps:

- First, define the architecture, including layers and activation functions.
- Start by initializing the network parameters (weights and biases).
- Run the forward pass to make the predictions.
- Then define the loss function for training.
- Integrate the network with the Fashion MNIST dataset for training purposes.

Define Neural Network Architecture

We will construct a simple feedforward neural network with two hidden layers, using the ReLU activation function for hidden layers and softmax for the output layer.

```
import jax

import jax.numpy as jnp

from jax import random
```

```
# Define the neural network architecture

def init_params(layer_sizes, key):

    """Initialize network parameters (weights and biases)
for each layer."""

    params = []

    for n_in, n_out in zip(layer_sizes[:-1],
layer_sizes[1:]):

        key, subkey = random.split(key)

        # Initialize weights with small random values

        weights = random.normal(subkey, (n_in, n_out)) *
0.01

        # Initialize biases with zeros

        biases = jnp.zeros(n_out)

        params.append((weights, biases))

    return params

# Define the layer sizes: input -> hidden1 -> hidden2 ->
output

layer_sizes = [28 * 28, 128, 64, 10]  # Input: 784,
Hidden1: 128, Hidden2: 64, Output: 10

# Random key for initialization

key = random.PRNGKey(0)

# Initialize parameters

params = init_params(layer_sizes, key)
```

In this setup, **layer_sizes** specifies the number of neurons in each layer, with 784 input features (28x28 flattened image), two hidden layers (128 and 64 neurons), and an output layer for 10 classes. We initialize the weights with small random values and biases as zeros.

Implement Forward Pass

The forward pass will compute the output of the network, given the input data. We will use ReLU activation for the hidden layers and a softmax function for the output layer.

```
def relu(x):
    """ReLU activation function."""
    return jnp.maximum(0, x)
def softmax(x):
    """Softmax activation function."""
    exp_x = jnp.exp(x - jnp.max(x))
    return exp_x / exp_x.sum(axis=1, keepdims=True)
def forward(params, x):
    """Perform a forward pass through the network."""
    # Flatten the input image
    x = x.reshape((x.shape[0], -1))
    # Loop over each layer
    for i, (weights, biases) in enumerate(params[:-1]):
        # Linear transformation
        x = jnp.dot(x, weights) + biases
        # Apply ReLU activation for hidden layers
        x = relu(x)
```

```
    # Final layer (output)
    final_weights, final_biases = params[-1]
    logits = jnp.dot(x, final_weights) + final_biases
    # Apply softmax activation to get probabilities
    return softmax(logits)
```

The **forward** function calculates the output of the network by sequentially applying linear transformations (matrix multiplication and bias addition) and activation functions to each layer.

Define Loss Function

We will use the cross-entropy loss to measure the difference between the predicted probabilities and the true labels.

```
def cross_entropy_loss(params, x, y):
    """Compute the cross-entropy loss."""
    preds = forward(params, x)
    # Convert labels to one-hot encoding
    y_one_hot = jax.nn.one_hot(y, num_classes=10)
    # Compute the average cross-entropy loss
    loss = -jnp.mean(jnp.sum(y_one_hot * jnp.log(preds +
1e-8), axis=1))
    return loss
```

In this function, we calculate the loss by computing the negative log of the predicted probabilities corresponding to the true labels and averaging it over the batch.

Implement Parameter Update using Gradient Descent

Next, we will update the parameters using stochastic gradient descent (SGD). We calculate the gradients of the loss function with respect to the parameters and update the weights and biases accordingly.

```
def sgd_update(params, grads, learning_rate):
    """Update parameters using SGD."""
    new_params = []
    for (w, b), (dw, db) in zip(params, grads):
        # Update weights and biases
        new_w = w - learning_rate * dw
        new_b = b - learning_rate * db
        new_params.append((new_w, new_b))
    return new_params
```

Train Neural Network

Now we can set up the training loop to train the model using the Fashion MNIST dataset.

```
learning_rate = 0.01
num_epochs = 10
# Function to compute gradients
grad_loss = jax.grad(cross_entropy_loss)
def train_network(train_ds, params, num_epochs):
    for epoch in range(num_epochs):
        epoch_loss = 0
        for batch in train_ds:
```

```
            images, labels = batch
            # Compute gradients
            grads = grad_loss(params, images, labels)
            # Update parameters
            params = sgd_update(params, grads,
learning_rate)
            # Compute batch loss
            batch_loss = cross_entropy_loss(params,
images, labels)
            epoch_loss += batch_loss
        print(f"Epoch {epoch + 1}, Loss: {epoch_loss}")
    return params
# Train the network
trained_params = train_network(train_ds, params,
num_epochs)
```

This training loop iterates over the dataset for a specified number of epochs, computes the gradients of the loss function with respect to the network parameters, updates the parameters using SGD, and prints the loss after each epoch.

Evaluate Trained Model

To evaluate the model's performance, we will use the test dataset to measure accuracy.

```
def compute_accuracy(params, test_ds):
    correct = 0
    total = 0
```

```
    for batch in test_ds:
        images, labels = batch
        # Perform the forward pass to get predictions
        preds = forward(params, images)
        # Get the predicted class by taking the argmax
        predicted_class = jnp.argmax(preds, axis=1)
        # Count correct predictions
        correct += jnp.sum(predicted_class == labels)
        total += labels.shape[0]
    accuracy = correct / total
    return accuracy
# Evaluate the trained model
accuracy = compute_accuracy(trained_params, test_ds)
print(f"Test Accuracy: {accuracy * 100:.2f}%")
```

This evaluation function computes the model's accuracy on the test dataset by comparing the predicted class with the true labels.

This solution showed us how to set up a training loop for the Fashion MNIST dataset and get a basic level of performance, which we can improve by using more advanced techniques like better initialization, regularization, and different optimization algorithms.

Training with Penzai

Managing machine learning experiments and tracking hyperparameters, metrics, and results systematically is crucial for optimizing model performance and ensuring reproducibility. When working with multiple models or tuning hyperparameters, it can be challenging to keep track of different runs and configurations manually. To address this issue, we will use Penzai, a tool designed for experiment tracking and management. In this recipe, we introduce Penzai and demonstrate how to integrate it into our JAX-based workflow, allowing us to log hyperparameters, metrics, and other important details during training, thus making experiments easier to monitor, compare, and reproduce.

About Penzai

Penzai is a lightweight and flexible tool for managing machine learning experiments, enabling the tracking of hyperparameters, metrics, and results. The process involves:

1. Installing Penzai and setting up a project.
2. Logging hyperparameters and metrics during the training process.
3. Using Penzai's visualization and comparison tools to analyze different experiment runs.
4. Ensuring reproducibility by saving all relevant experiment details.

Installing Penzai

Just a heads-up, you'll want to make sure Penzai is installed on your system. If you don't have it yet, you can add it using:

```
pip install penzai
```

Next, initialize a new Penzai project. This step creates a configuration file to manage experiment metadata.

```
penzai init --project-name "Fashion MNIST Training"
```

This command sets up a new project named "Fashion MNIST Training" and creates the necessary configuration files. You can also set up storage backends or cloud integration options if required.

Configuring Penzai in Training Script

To integrate Penzai into your JAX training script, start by importing the Penzai module and initializing a new experiment run.

```
import penzai

# Initialize Penzai

penzai.init(project="Fashion MNIST Training")
```

```
# Start a new experiment run

run = penzai.start_run(run_name="Baseline Model
Training")
```

The **`start_run`** function begins a new experiment, allowing us to log hyperparameters, metrics, and results associated with this run.

Logging Hyperparameters

Before starting the training, log the relevant hyperparameters such as learning rate, batch size, and number of epochs.

```
# Hyperparameters

learning_rate = 0.01

batch_size = 128

num_epochs = 10

# Log hyperparameters

run.log_hyperparams({

    "learning_rate": learning_rate,

    "batch_size": batch_size,

    "num_epochs": num_epochs

})
```

This step ensures that the key settings for the experiment are recorded, enabling you to refer back to them when reviewing or reproducing the run.

Logging Training Metrics

As the training progresses, log important metrics like loss and accuracy at each epoch. This allows Penzai to track the performance of the model over time.

```
def train_network_with_tracking(train_ds, params,
num_epochs):

    for epoch in range(num_epochs):

        epoch_loss = 0

        for batch in train_ds:

            images, labels = batch

            # Compute gradients

            grads = jax.grad(cross_entropy_loss)(params,
images, labels)

            # Update parameters

            params = sgd_update(params, grads,
learning_rate)

            # Compute batch loss

            batch_loss = cross_entropy_loss(params,
images, labels)

            epoch_loss += batch_loss


        # Log the epoch loss

        run.log_metric("epoch_loss", epoch_loss,
step=epoch)

        # Optionally, log additional metrics

        accuracy = compute_accuracy(params, test_ds)

        run.log_metric("accuracy", accuracy, step=epoch)
```

```
        print(f"Epoch {epoch + 1}, Loss: {epoch_loss},
Accuracy: {accuracy * 100:.2f}%")


    return params

# Train the network while logging metrics

trained_params = train_network_with_tracking(train_ds,
params, num_epochs)
```

By logging metrics such as loss and accuracy at each epoch, you can visualize the model's learning curve in Penzai's dashboard.

Visualizing and Comparing Experiments

After logging metrics, use Penzai's web interface to analyze the training progress, compare different runs, and observe trends.

Open the Penzai dashboard:

```
penzai ui
```

Then, view the experiments listed under "Fashion MNIST Training" and compare metrics such as loss and accuracy across different runs. You can also use built-in tools to create plots that show how metrics evolve over time or how different hyperparameter settings affect the results.

Logging Model Artifacts for Reproducibility

Apart from tracking metrics and hyperparameters, it is important to save model artifacts (e.g., trained parameters) for reproducibility and further analysis.

```
# Save trained model parameters

model_artifact_path = "model_params.pkl"

with open(model_artifact_path, "wb") as f:

    import pickle
```

```
    pickle.dump(trained_params, f)

# Log the model artifact

run.log_artifact(model_artifact_path)
```

Logging artifacts like the trained model's weights makes sure that you can recreate the experiment or make some improvements if needed.

Ending Experiment Run

After completing the training and logging the necessary information, make sure to end the experiment run.

```
run.end()
```

This finalizes the current experiment, allowing you to start a new run or analyze the completed experiments in Penzai.

By incorporating Penzai into the training process, we efficiently managed our experiments, systematically tracked hyperparameters, and logged metrics for evaluating model performance. Penzai's ability to visualize training progress, compare different runs, and save model artifacts facilitates reproducibility and optimization of machine learning projects.

Evaluating and Visualizing Model Performance

Assessing a machine learning model's learning progress is essential for understanding its effectiveness and identifying areas for improvement. In JAX-based workflows, it can be challenging to implement evaluation metrics and visualize the model's training and testing performance without high-level libraries. To address this, we will use evaluation metrics such as accuracy, precision, recall, and confusion matrices, along with visualization tools like Matplotlib, to track the model's progress and gain insights into its behavior during training. This recipe demonstrates how to implement these techniques to monitor the performance of the JAX model we have developed so far.

Here, to evaluate and visualize the model's performance effectively, we will:

1. Implement standard evaluation metrics such as accuracy, precision, recall, and confusion matrix.
2. Visualize the model's learning curves by plotting metrics like loss and accuracy over time.

3. Use confusion matrices to identify where the model is making correct and incorrect predictions.
4. Integrate these evaluation techniques into the JAX training and testing workflow.

Implement Evaluation Metrics

To start, we will implement common evaluation metrics, focusing on accuracy, precision, recall, and confusion matrix calculation.

```
import jax.numpy as jnp

def compute_accuracy(params, test_ds):

    """Calculate the accuracy of the model on the test
dataset."""

    correct = 0

    total = 0

    for batch in test_ds:

        images, labels = batch

        # Perform the forward pass to get predictions

        preds = forward(params, images)

        # Get the predicted class by taking the argmax

        predicted_class = jnp.argmax(preds, axis=1)

        # Count correct predictions

        correct += jnp.sum(predicted_class == labels)

        total += labels.shape[0]

    accuracy = correct / total

    return accuracy
```

```
def compute_precision_recall(params, test_ds,
num_classes=10):
    """Calculate precision and recall for each class."""
    true_positives = jnp.zeros(num_classes)
    false_positives = jnp.zeros(num_classes)
    false_negatives = jnp.zeros(num_classes)

    for batch in test_ds:
        images, labels = batch
        preds = forward(params, images)
        predicted_class = jnp.argmax(preds, axis=1)

        for i in range(num_classes):
            true_positives =
true_positives.at[i].add(jnp.sum((predicted_class == i) &
(labels == i)))
            false_positives =
false_positives.at[i].add(jnp.sum((predicted_class == i)
& (labels != i)))
            false_negatives =
false_negatives.at[i].add(jnp.sum((predicted_class != i)
& (labels == i)))

    # Compute precision and recall
```

```
    precision = true_positives / (true_positives +
false_positives + 1e-8)

    recall = true_positives / (true_positives +
false_negatives + 1e-8)


    return precision, recall
```

The **compute_accuracy** function calculates the overall accuracy, while the **compute_precision_recall** function calculates precision and recall for each class, providing more detailed performance insights.

Compute Confusion Matrix

A confusion matrix can help visualize the model's performance across different classes by showing where the model is making correct and incorrect predictions.

```
def compute_confusion_matrix(params, test_ds,
num_classes=10):

    """Compute the confusion matrix for the test
dataset."""

    confusion_matrix = jnp.zeros((num_classes,
num_classes))


    for batch in test_ds:

        images, labels = batch

        preds = forward(params, images)

        predicted_class = jnp.argmax(preds, axis=1)
```

```
        for true_label, pred_label in zip(labels,
predicted_class):

            confusion_matrix =
confusion_matrix.at[true_label, pred_label].add(1)


    return confusion_matrix
```

The confusion matrix will help identify patterns in the model's errors, indicating which classes the model confuses with each other.

Visualize Training Progress

To understand how the model improves over time, plot the training and validation loss and accuracy for each epoch. We will use Matplotlib for visualization.

```
import matplotlib.pyplot as plt

def plot_learning_curves(training_losses,
validation_accuracies):

    """Plot the learning curves for loss and accuracy."""

    epochs = range(1, len(training_losses) + 1)


    # Plot training loss

    plt.figure(figsize=(12, 5))

    plt.subplot(1, 2, 1)

    plt.plot(epochs, training_losses, label='Training
Loss')

    plt.xlabel('Epoch')
```

```
    plt.ylabel('Loss')
    plt.title('Training Loss Over Time')
    plt.legend()
    # Plot validation accuracy
    plt.subplot(1, 2, 2)
    plt.plot(epochs, validation_accuracies,
label='Validation Accuracy')
    plt.xlabel('Epoch')
    plt.ylabel('Accuracy')
    plt.title('Validation Accuracy Over Time')
    plt.legend()

    plt.show()
# Example data for demonstration
training_losses = [0.9, 0.7, 0.5, 0.3, 0.2]  # Dummy loss
values
validation_accuracies = [0.70, 0.75, 0.80, 0.85, 0.88]  #
Dummy accuracy values
# Plot the learning curves
plot_learning_curves(training_losses,
validation_accuracies)
```

These plots help visualize the trends in loss reduction and accuracy improvement during training, providing insight into the model's learning process.

Visualize Confusion Matrix

Visualizing the confusion matrix helps in understanding the types of mistakes the model makes.

```
import seaborn as sns

def plot_confusion_matrix(conf_matrix, class_names):

    """Plot the confusion matrix using Seaborn."""

    plt.figure(figsize=(10, 8))

    sns.heatmap(conf_matrix, annot=True, fmt="d",
cmap="Blues", xticklabels=class_names,
yticklabels=class_names)

    plt.xlabel('Predicted Label')

    plt.ylabel('True Label')

    plt.title('Confusion Matrix')

    plt.show()

# Example class names for Fashion MNIST

class_names = [

    'T-shirt/top', 'Trouser', 'Pullover', 'Dress',
'Coat',

    'Sandal', 'Shirt', 'Sneaker', 'Bag', 'Ankle boot'

]

# Compute the confusion matrix

conf_matrix = compute_confusion_matrix(trained_params,
test_ds, num_classes=10)

# Plot the confusion matrix
```

```
plot_confusion_matrix(conf_matrix, class_names)
```

The heatmap representation of the confusion matrix reveals which classes the model struggles to distinguish, indicating areas for potential improvement.

Automating Evaluation after each Epoch

To monitor the model's learning progress systematically, integrate evaluation and visualization within the training loop.

```
def train_and_evaluate(train_ds, test_ds, params,
num_epochs):

    training_losses = []

    validation_accuracies = []

    for epoch in range(num_epochs):

        # Training phase

        epoch_loss = 0

        for batch in train_ds:

            images, labels = batch

            grads = jax.grad(cross_entropy_loss)(params,
images, labels)

            params = sgd_update(params, grads,
learning_rate)

            batch_loss = cross_entropy_loss(params,
images, labels)

            epoch_loss += batch_loss
```

```
        # Log the training loss
        training_losses.append(epoch_loss)
        # Evaluation phase
        accuracy = compute_accuracy(params, test_ds)
        validation_accuracies.append(accuracy)

        # Print epoch summary
        print(f"Epoch {epoch + 1}, Loss: {epoch_loss},
Validation Accuracy: {accuracy * 100:.2f}%")
    # Plot learning curves after training
    plot_learning_curves(training_losses,
validation_accuracies)
    # Compute and plot the confusion matrix after the
final epoch
    conf_matrix = compute_confusion_matrix(params,
test_ds, num_classes=10)
    plot_confusion_matrix(conf_matrix, class_names)
    return params
# Train the network and evaluate its performance
trained_params = train_and_evaluate(train_ds, test_ds,
params, num_epochs)
```

This integrated training and evaluation approach enables real-time monitoring of the model's performance, providing valuable insights throughout the training process.

We used metrics like accuracy, precision, recall, and confusion matrices, along with visualizing learning curves and confusion matrices, to keep a closer eye on how the model was doing. These techniques helped us understand how the model was learning and also showed us where we could make it better. This made the process of developing the model more iterative and data-driven.

Summary

In short, we effectively trained neural networks and addressed the practical challenges we encountered along the way. We solved the data loading bottlenecks by leveraging TensorFlow Datasets to load and preprocess large datasets efficiently. Next, we built a neural network from scratch, giving you a hands-on understanding of how to construct layers, implement activation functions, and configure parameter updates directly in JAX.

The chapter also introduced the use of Penzai for systematic experiment tracking, which enabled the logging of hyperparameters, metrics, and results during training. Furthermore, we examined techniques for evaluating the model's learning progress. We focused on implementing evaluation metrics such as accuracy, precision, and recall, as well as using confusion matrices to analyze model predictions in detail.

Index

Epilogue

As we reach the conclusion of Google JAX Cookbook, I'm filled with excitement as I reflect on how the techniques and solutions covered here are more than just theoretical exercises. These amazing tools are ready for you to use every day in your machine learning and AI projects! These recipes will empower you to build a new model from scratch, optimize existing pipelines, and debug tricky runtime issues with confidence!

The wonderful thing about day-to-day work in machine learning and AI is that it's often unpredictable! You might encounter slow computation speeds, memory constraints, unexpected bugs, or the need to fine-tune a model to achieve higher performance—and you'll be ready for them! These situations call for more than just familiarity with the tools. They demand the ability to apply them effectively to solve real problems! This book is here to give you that problem-solving mindset you need to succeed! And the best part is, you can learn so much more than just how to write faster code! They're about so much more than just writing faster code! You'll gain a deeper understanding of how numerical computation can be optimized, how hardware constraints can be managed, and how modern libraries like JAX can transform the way you approach machine learning. You've explored techniques for efficient data loading, ways to use mixed precision for training speed, methods to monitor model performance in real-time, and strategies to distribute computation across specialized hardware. Each of these skills will make your day-to-day tasks more streamlined and less error-prone!

The tips on profiling, debugging, serialization, and experiment tracking will help you stay agile as you grow projects or change direction. You've picked up some tips on how to avoid common mistakes, integrate external functions without any hiccups, and keep your projects stable and reproducible. This kind of knowledge doesn't just solve one problem; it changes the way you approach all your work.

The recipes are designed to not only provide solutions but also to get you more engaged with the tools you have at your disposal. I hope that, with the insights from this book, you'll find your daily work less of a chore and more of an opportunity to innovate and push the boundaries of what's possible in AI. As you continue to develop, optimize, and deploy your models, may these recipes serve as reliable companions, guiding you toward better and faster results in all your machine learning projects.

Thank You

www.ingramcontent.com/pod-product-compliance
Lightning Source LLC
Chambersburg PA
CBHW080211170726
48282CB00030B/1073
9788197950414